DIRTY SECRETS,
DIRTY LIES

Dirty Secrets, Dirty Lies: Escape the Web of Deceit That Holds You Back is a must read for today's Christian leader. If you want to help others, this book will arm you with Biblical insight and practical tools for life-changing ministry success.

—**David Gibbs III**, President and General Counsel of the National Center for Life and Liberty

It is not often that a book arrests my attention as completely as Ray Traylor's *Dirty Secrets, Dirty Lies: Escape the Web of Deceit That Holds You Back*. With refreshing candor and forthrightness, Mr. Traylor tackles perhaps the most common sin of this facile media driven age: addiction to unhealthy excesses. Pornography, in particular, is epidemic among Christians today. Parents need to read *Dirty Secrets* with their teenage children and discuss it around the kitchen table. Every church should have a annual topical Bible study and use *Dirty Secrets* as its study guide. Problems that Mr. Traylor examines will not go away without radical interventions. We all owe Mr. Traylor a debt of gratitude for sensitively addressing these problems and for offering sensible solutions. I hope you will pick up your copy today.

—**Dr. James Stobaugh**, President of For Such a Time As This Ministries

Dirty Secrets, Dirty Lies does more than identify "besetting sins" — it points men to the only solution for sin: Christ. Through practical insights and suggestions, Ray Traylor presents a biblical path to purity. I highly recommend this book for all men.

—**Scott Attebery**, Executive Director at DiscipleGuide Church Resources; Baptist Missionary Association of America

What a timely book for a compromised Christian culture! Ray balances personal transparency with passionate appeal to the life not plagued by besetting sins, arranging the Scriptures with insightful wisdom and loving exhortation to encourage you to overcome. You've got to get this book!Ray Traylor's gifted writing style pierces through the challenging issues facing us today as we strive to live a Godly life in a hurting, broken world. Allow the insights and concrete steps outlined in this book to elevate your daily living and transform your life as you discover the faith, truth and power to live a "life overcoming." The wisdom and knowledge packed within the pages of this inspiring book will equip you with the tools to act on faith and face the future with strength and purpose.

—**Beth Anne Rankin**, Former Miss Arkansas, Christian Radio Talk Show Co-Host, Teacher and Conference Leader for Women's Ministry and Former Policy Advisor to the National Governors Association.

Ray Traylor's book *Dirty Secrets, Dirty Lies* is a fascinating book about how to overcome besetting sins. He doesn't describe a step-by-step program, but rather a practical and transformational process based on the Word of God to free you from your obstacles and excel in the Christian life! I urge you to get your copy today!

—**Jacob Ricker**, Founder of Never Thirst, a relief agency bringing water and Christ's love to disaster victims

DIRTY SECRETS

ESCAPE THE WEB OF DECEIT THAT HOLDS YOU BACK

DIRTY LIES

RAY TRAYLOR

New York

DIRTY SECRETS, DIRTY LIES
ESCAPE THE WEB OF DECEIT THAT HOLDS YOU BACK

© 2014 RAY TRAYLOR.

Published in New York, New York, by Morgan James Publishing. Morgan James and The Entrepreneurial Publisher are trademarks of Morgan James, LLC. www.MorganJamesPublishing.com

The Morgan James Speakers Group can bring authors to your live event. For more information or to book an event visit The Morgan James Speakers Group at www.TheMorganJamesSpeakersGroup.com.

The New American Standard Bible is version used in the text unless otherwise noted.

ISBN 978-1-61448-519-3 paperback
ISBN 978-1-61448-863-7 hard cover
ISBN 978-1-61448-520-9 eBook
ISBN 978-1-61448-521-6 audio
Library of Congress Control Number:
2012955666

BitLit
FOR ALL THE BOOKS YOU OWN

FREE eBook edition for your existing eReader with purchase

PRINT NAME ABOVE

For more information, instructions, restrictions, and to register your copy, go to **www.bitlit.ca/readers/register** or use your QR Reader to scan the barcode:

Cover Design by:
Rachel Lopez
www.r2cdesign.com

Interior Design by:
Bonnie Bushman
bonnie@caboodlegraphics.com

In an effort to support local communities, raise awareness and funds, Morgan James Publishing donates a percentage of all book sales for the life of each book to Habitat for Humanity Peninsula and Greater Williamsburg.

Get involved today, visit
www.MorganJamesBuilds.com

Habitat for Humanity®
Peninsula and Greater Williamsburg
Building Partner

Table of Contents

Foreword

by Tony Meggs,
President and CEO of Christian Care Ministry

No matter how you look at it, today we are living in a culture of ever increasing sinfulness, moral decay and relational rot. The church is no longer at the center of influence, and we live in what can best be described as a post-Christian America. We are taught in Galatians 6:7 that we should not deceive ourselves and that God will not be mocked. We are told that man will reap what he sows. Fortunately, God is patient and longsuffering… but for how long?

The church today is not the church of our fathers. It is safe to say that the world's opinion of Christians has changed because the Christian community changed. The same moral decay that exists in the broader culture is all too often found in the lives of many Christians. The same relational rot that is destroying America has spread too far and too deep into the everyday lives of Christian families. Pick your poison: adultery, deceit, selfishness, pornography, materialism, gluttony or idolatry. These are just a few examples of the sinfulness that has led to our nation's downfall. These same poisons are too easily found within the walls of the Church and at the center of Christian families. The result is broken families, ruined relationships, and shattered lives. Over the last century, the divorce rate in the U.S. has increased by more than 300%. More surprising, is the fact that divorce among Christians is actually higher today than that of their atheist/agnostic counterparts. Since 1950, the number of children being raised by a single mom has increased 1,350% for whites and 341% for blacks. The consequences of sin have taken a toll and have forever damaged the souls of the next generation.

Our country is suffering from a lack of an authentic Christian presence. While many claim the Christian moniker and label, few seem to live out a life of true commitment and obedience. Too many worship at the feet of "materialism", the false god which enslaves. The result has been a ridiculous explosion of household debt that leaves people exposed and vulnerable to the whims of market gyrations. And when the recent housing bubble popped many found themselves in bondage of their debtors. This combined with the current declines in incomes and increases in joblessness only amplifies this sense of hopelessness.

An authentic Christian community should be the beacon in this current darkness. Yet, we find ourselves ill-equipped, even floundering in our faith, when the pressure is applied. We are quick to pile on more layers to our sin problems through guilt and shame. We lack the faith to let God handle our problems and guide our thoughts and plans. We are dishonest with ourselves and with God. As a result, our prayers go unanswered, and we miss God's blessings and favor.

The bottom line is that Christians need some direction and hope, now more than ever, during these challenging times. Ray Traylor is just that hope. His insight is just what the Christian community is searching for—real answers based on Scripture. This book is a roadmap, a guide for escaping the web of deceit which leads to sin and death.

I have been fortunate to know and work with Ray Traylor over the last five years. He serves selflessly on the Board of Directors for Christian Care Ministry where I have seen firsthand a man who loves the Lord and lives his life with integrity, according to the Scriptures. He is one to guide with wisdom and discernment, and most importantly, humility. His unfailing commitment to serving the members of Christian Care Ministry is to be applauded. My relationship with Ray has grown outside the boardroom where I have seen him mentor and teach others through his first book, *True Riches.*

As you open up this book today, I encourage you to pray about how the Lord will use it and you to influence the culture. Signs are that things aren't going to get better—in fact, I often wonder just how much worse it will get before Christ returns. As the sin in our culture and in our churches accelerates, we see a climate ripe for discontentment, strife and discord. The Baby Boomers are at the end of their ropes, settling for less and fighting the Millennials for a coveted job. The Millennials are resentful of those that came before them, allegedly mismanaging their future. Our current generation's only hope to escape the sin which is ever growing in our culture is to learn to totally rely upon Christ, and on Christ alone!

Time is drawing near, and we need to be the light for this dark world. Today, more than ever, there is a sense of urgency about our future. None of us knows the day or the hour of Christ's return, and we don't want to be caught distracted from our true purpose. Instead of waiting for His return with a sense of resignation, why don't we gather our resources and commit to His cause? Let us be the movement that turns the world around. Let us be the light in this dark world, the hope in this hopeless place and the righteousness among sinners. Let us take back this world for Jesus. Picking up this book today is a great place to start.

U.S. Divorce Rates (last 100 Years)

1. Divorce Among Christians Higher than Atheist/Agnostics
   http://www.barna.org/family-kids-articles/42-new-marriage-and-divorce-statistics-released?q=divorce+rates

2. Rise is single Mom Families http://papundits.wordpress.com/2012/07/14/dogs-instead -of-children/

Introduction

The End is the Result of the Process

Freddie is a middle-aged man with a successful career, great family, and a bright future as a CEO of a successful high-tech company. Until recently, he actually appeared to be a classic model of the American success story. His only problem is that he found himself in the hospital. He was not afflicted with the expected ailments of a man of his age... not diabetes, heart attack, heart disease or even cancer. Freddie has been diagnosed as HIV positive. Unfortunately, he has a lot of explaining to do. You see, Freddie had a much bigger problem than HIV. He has something the old timers called a "besetting sin". HIV was merely a symptom of his hidden addiction to pornography. His porn addiction led Freddie to a life of sexual compromise.

Like most men in his generation, he got hooked on porn as a teenager. The cultural revolution of the 60s, 70s and 80s made porn more and more accessible. Freddie did not realize that indulging in his dirty secret would result in such devastation to his health, family, and career. He had been allured by the pleasure that comes from tasting the forbidden fruit, the thrill of the new experience, and the heightened sensation of experimentation. He knew his addiction to porn was against his values, but he felt trapped and helpless to resist it. It seemed to be everywhere around him. All his buddies had the same problem, and it just didn't seem so bad when he saw that other people were doing it too.

But, there were times when he felt awful about his porn addiction. He felt like he was the worst husband and father in the world. If his wife and kids knew about the porn, they would lose all respect for him and his life would be over. He felt he had to cover it up or lose everything.

Whenever he went to church, which seemed to be less and less as the years rolled by, he felt the pastor must have known about his secret. In every message, he was reminded of his sexual sins. His pastor, the one person he felt could help him, was so intolerant of pornography that he felt he would not get an understanding ear. Thus, seeking out spiritual help really did not seem to be a viable option.

Early in his Christian experience, he heard that Christ could give victory over addictions, but no one ever explained how to overcome a tough and continuing sin. So, he developed two theories. Either a person had to muster a vast amount of self-control to be an overcomer, or a person had to have a strange miracle from God which would take away the desire. Neither of those approaches seemed to work for Freddie, so he finally stopped trying to resist. He felt that there was no hope in overcoming the allurement of porn and quietly settled into a life of defeat. Not everyone is addicted to porn, but there are plenty of other "besetting sins" which pull people into a constant cycle of defeat. This book is about overcoming besetting sins. Examples of these include overeating, gossip, lying, stealing, abusive speech and many others too numerous to mention here. A besetting sin is like a virus on our computer—the computer is trapped into repeating the same mistake over and over again. A besetting sin is like a winter head cold which keeps coming back—we never seem to get rid of it. A besetting sin is a bad habit, but it is more serious. A bad habit might be annoying because we keep doing what we don't want to do. A besetting sin is more than annoying; it is destructive because it harms our lives and our relationships.

A Common Problem with No Hope for a Different Outcome

The frailty of our human condition is played out over and over again. We have great goals, but we lack the strength or will to live up to our hopes and values. We try and fail.—Eventually, we give up and resign ourselves to a life of defeat. No hope or help seems available. Sadly, we miss out on one of the most powerful tools for success.

This book, *Dirty Secrets, Dirty Lies*, is a practical biblical guide to help us overcome whatever besetting sin we might be facing. Jesus very clearly states that there is hope and escape for any sin which confronts us, "You shall know the truth and the truth shall set you free." The solution begins with Christ, His promises, and the practical principles found in the scriptures that give us victory over any temptation we are facing.

The Solution

Most people think that they need more self-control, but the Scriptures teach something else. We need to change the focus of our thoughts and actions. The Bible teaches us to redirect our hearts and minds. We need to move from merely avoiding the negative to accentuating the positive, thus replacing the wrong thoughts and actions with the right thoughts and actions. This approach can be summed up in the question, "Am I reacting to the temptations of life or being proactive to live a godly life." The goal and motivation of the experience is totally reversed. Our "want to" changes and the power to be an overcomer becomes abundant as these biblical principles are understood and practiced. I have observed the learning and development process in my own life and in the lives of hundreds of others. The truth can really set us free when we put it into practice.

The New Life

The way to overcome a besetting sin is to totally redirect our focus. Most Christians are reacting to whatever the world throws their way, and they are usually defeated in the process. That is just the opposite of what is available to any child of God. God wants His people to be ones who shape the culture, who introduce the right solution into any moral dilemma, and who lead the charge for the causes of the Kingdom of God.

Discover What God has Made Available to You

This book is for you if you have ever been defeated by a besetting sin. Maybe you're a guy who lies as easy as breathing. Maybe you've got sticky fingers and just can't resist swiping something, anytime you get a chance. Maybe you have never really passed a test on your own, but established an elaborate a plan for cheating your way through college. Maybe you can't resist that third piece of cheese cake—let alone that first piece. Maybe you can't pass on that second glance at that good looking woman. Maybe resisting that ice cold "Bud" or a drag on a joint is just beyond you. You can substitute whatever vice you have in this list. If you want real help with issues like these, then this book is for you. We'll examine the motivations behind the actions, the results of the actions, and how to tap into Christ's unlimited power supply.

Don't Put This Book Down

You've already started on a path to healing by looking at this book. It will give you the knowledge, wisdom, and secrets you have always wanted. You and others can start your lives again. Keep reading, and you will discover that you can overcome any temptation that comes along. Your lifestyle and character will be transformed into the man or woman God destined you to be.

For a free video summary of this chapter by the author go online to www.dirtysecretsdirtylies.com and click on Free Videos.

Nothing New Under the Sun

When We Are in the Dark—We Can't See

Do you remember Ted Haggard? Many years ago Ted was a rising star in the evangelical world. He was quite a powerhouse. Haggard was the pastor of New Life Church, a church with 10,000 members in Colorado Springs. He was also the President of the National Association of Evangelicals. He associated with President George W. Bush and other political leaders. The problem was that Ted had an issue that sabotaged his life. He had at least one male lover and an involvement with drugs. When he was discovered, everyone wondered: How could someone function effectively as a leader of God's people with those besetting sins?

Not only was Ted having sin issues, he wasn't willing to confess his problems to others. He did not begin the process of repentance until others discovered his problems. In a sensational news report of 2006, Haggard admitted to his deviant lifestyle and resigned as a pastor and the President of the National Association of Evangelicals. This scenario reminds me of Jesus' words,

> This is the judgment, that the Light has come into the world, and men loved the darkness rather than the Light, for their deeds were evil. For everyone who does evil hates the Light, and does not come to the Light for fear that his deeds will be exposed."
>
> **John 3:19–20**

Here Jesus is cutting through the fog of our denials and our excuses. According to Jesus, the real issue is that humans love evil and darkness, because if we were to love the light we would be exposed for what we really are... lovers of evil.

With that said, you're probably thinking. "What a distressing and hopeless thought! People love evil; they are also ashamed of that evil and want to cover it up. We might want to be more "positive" about human nature, but this is how Jesus looks at our situation.

If humans are really that mixed up, is there any hope of change? Can human nature be transformed and can people really live like saints? These are the core issues of this book.

The Devil is Not Very Creative

Even though Haggard's story was new at the time it happened, it had been played out millions of times before down through the ages. Even from the early history of God's dealing with mankind the problem of sin, blame shifting, denial, and cover up have all been in play. (To see the original case study read Genesis 3:1–13) Up to this point I have only introduced the besetting sin issue. There is still another element of this process we need to discuss. Specifically, there is a spiritual dimension. The spiritual dimension is a real and present threat in the likelihood of overcoming our besetting sins. The devil, Satan by name, was in the middle of it from the earliest annals of recorded history. Since those days his strategy hasn't changed. We conclude that the devil is not very creative. Why should he be? Why change what's working? Or is it somehow different now?

Strategy, Tactics and Technology

I enjoy reading history. It is a wonderful way to learn without the first hand pain usually associated with learning. Most of us don't learn that way. We primarily learn our lessons as my dad used to say, "…through the school of hard knocks." I've certainly learned many lessons the hard way. More and more I am interested in learning from the mistakes and successes of others. Let me give you an example of what we can learn from history.

One of the greatest military geniuses of history was Alexander the Great. He had an incredible mind for strategy. In his battle at Arbela (also known as Gaugamela), Alexander employed a battle strategy known today as envelopment.

The strategy was probably not original with Alexander, but we know from historical records that when he used it, he was very successful. It is also reported that Hannibal was very successful in using this strategy at the Battle of Cannae in 216 B.C.

The tactic behind envelopment is to engage the enemy's attention with a small but fierce secondary force on the front lines. This force is significantly weaker than the enemy's force thus creating a false hope of easy victory. The attack is not taken seriously, but is strong enough to get the attention of the enemy's leadership. While the small battle is raging, a much larger force envelops the flank and rear of the enemy cutting communication and supply lines forcing the enemy to engage a two front battle. This strategy also cuts off the enemy's line of retreat.

This strategy enabled Alexander to handily defeat Darius in 331 B.C., thus allowing him to ultimately capture Babylon. This strategy has been repeated through history. Robert E. Lee, an astute military strategist, employed the envelopment strategy, defeating the Union forces at Chancellorsville during the U.S. Civil War in 1863. In 1942, German general, Erwin Rommel used this strategy to defeat Allied forces at Gazala in North Africa, leading to the capture of the port of Tobruk.

Even though the strategy has not changed, the technology of war was different in the various situations. In Alexander's case, foot soldiers were used. In Lee's case, the cavalry and canons were used. In Rommel's case, tanks were used.

The devil's strategies to trap and to defeat people are always the same, but the technological tools which he uses vary from generation to generation. Today's technology makes it easier to participate in dirty secrets and dirty lies. The devil uses the same old temptations, but today's internet and electronics give a new twist to his old work.

We Cannot Count on Being Lucky

For the gate is small and the way is narrow that leads to life, and there are few who find it."

Mathew 7:14

It may seem surprising to most people, but according to Jesus there will be few who find eternal life and who overcome the sin which beleaguers them. Jesus also said it in another way

"… "Truly, truly, I say to you, everyone who commits sin is the slave of sin. So if the Son makes you free, you will be free indeed."

John 8:34 and 36

The message of the Bible is "If we let 'nature take its course,' then we are enslaved to sin." Then we are in deep trouble. We do not know how to live, and we do not have the power to escape the death in our lives. Paul said in

"And you were dead in your trespasses and sins, in which you formerly walked according to the course of this world, according to the prince of the power of the air, of the spirit that is now working in the sons of disobedience."

Ephesians 2:1, 2

We are trapped by problems—not minor problems, but an absolute and serious condition in our souls. The Bible calls it slavery to sin. We long to live, but there is deadness in our souls. Everyone is trapped by this general condition of sin, but some of us are trapped by a constant and an overwhelming sin of a particular kind. Over the years I have counseled with hundreds of people who could not overcome their besetting sins. This slavery to a particular sin causes all sorts of dysfunctions within the person. It creates a conflict that the person is never able to overcome. Without God in a person's life, the power to overcome such a sin is impossible. Most people never learn how to overcome their temptations. Their struggle with a besetting sin never seems to end.

Modern Psychology Has Failed to Fix the Problem

When faced with "bad habits," people often turn to psychologists for help. Modern psychology has failed to fix the sin problem.

Of course, for millennia philosophers and polymaths have been presenting ideas about how to fix this problem, certainly to no avail. Modern psychology has its direct roots in the teaching of prominent philosophers of the enlightenment era, which were highly influenced by the Greek philosophers Thales, Plato and Aristotle. Some of the earliest philosophers of the era include Baruch Spinoza, John Locke and Pierre Bayle. These men laid the foundation of the enlightenment philosophy which was furthered by the likes of Voltaire and Montesquieu. These philosophers purported the theory of the Tabula Rasa which declares that individuals are born without built-in mental content. It teaches that their knowledge comes from experience and perception as opposed to their genetic or spiritual makeup.

These philosophers had a profound impact on the next generation of intellectual influencers from which modern psychological theory has emanated. The most noted of the next generation psychologists based much of their psychological understanding on the works of the proceeding philosophers. These noted psychologists of this era were Wilhelm Wundt, William James, Sigmund Freud and his heir apparent Carl Jung. Freudian thought dominated the discipline of psychology through the first half of the 20th century until the 1950s. During the 1950s, a new viewpoint of psychology called behaviorism became the dominant school of thought. Behaviorism first championed by J. B. Watson and others, later along with B. F. Skinner, changed the entire psychological approach. Each of these psychologists developed their own following and their trainees usually built on the understanding of their predecessors or rejected their ideals. At this point in modern psychological counseling, behavioral issues still remain. Now, new psychological books are continuously being released to the public. All of them are variations on the themes developed from the philosophers of the enlightenment period and behavioral psychology. Today some of the world's most noted psychological practitioners readily admit that very little lasting behavior change is made through psychological counseling. In a video interview posted June 27, 2011 on youtube. com psychology professor Michael J. Lambert, PhD noted that roughly 8% of people involved in psychotherapy get worse and about 40% don't change one way or another. So if this conclusion is true and the results are so poor, why are we still trying the same methods that are not working?

Psychologist tell us that experience, conditioning, and perception play major factors in the behavior of the individual, but this is in stark contrast to the teaching of scripture and observation of human nature and behavior. The Bible teaches that there is a fundamental flaw in human nature which only God can correct. The world is full of psychologists, but we still have behavioral issues that aren't getting better. Counselors want to reassure us that with a greater knowledge of ourselves, our past, our situation today, our potential along with other factors we can overcome whatever we are facing. They do not help us honestly face our brokenness, our need for God's grace, our need for God's wisdom, and our need for God's church.

Forgotten Truths—Ephesians 4

This book offers a new approach for modern Christians, but it is really an old approach. We need to return to some basic truths found in the Bible. Our approach will be "new" because it is an approach which is new to us.

Actually, the United States of America was founded by people who used this approach. The founding fathers of the United States were rooted in Christian, Biblical teaching. These colonies were founded by people seeking religious freedom. They rewrote the laws and standards based on the Old Testament teachings of the nation of Israel. We have a constant reference of Scriptural teaching from the Mayflower Compact down through the end of the 19th century. These Biblical concepts were gradually displaced over the past 100 years as the predominately Christian population was replaced by an agnostic population.

The apostle Paul specifically outlined the way to have victory over every besetting sin. The principles are explained in Ephesians chapter four with examples given to illuminate the subject. Later in the book we will go into great detail on how to do that.

Are You Going to be a Winner or Loser?

A besetting sin is a losing battle—at least without outside help. There are some temptations which have very little power over us (at least at this point in our lives). In contrast a besetting sin is a temptation which seems so strong that we feel we cannot win. It is a situation or thought where victory seems impossible. We feel like losers.

Why not be a winner? To be a winner we must make a conscious choice. When faced with almost certain defeat, we wonder: "Why should I even try?"

We all have various motivating factors. Some of the ones that really challenged me had to do with the quality of my life. You may think that seems strange, but you know, that really is our motivation most of the time. Jesus said that He came to give an abundant life to His followers in John 10:10. Why do so few people experience this abundant life?

In John 10:10, Jesus promised to give his disciples abundant, full lives. We can have lives filled with peace, joy, and satisfaction, if we carefully listen to and obey what God tells us in the Bible. Sadly, many Christians do not feel that peace, joy, and satisfaction. Here are three reasons why people do not live the abundant life which Jesus promised:

1. Many Christians do not think that a life of satisfaction is possible. Just as some people give up on finding a happy marriage, many give up on finding the abundant life which Jesus promised. They don't believe it is possible, because

they have never met anyone who regularly experiences that abundant life. However, just because your experiences have not been great, does that mean that it is not possible to have an abundant life? In this book we'll explore the details of how to experience the abundant life.

2. Some Christians don't think it is worth the trouble it takes to learn the lessons. Walking with God and following His principles in our daily lives does take time, patience, and training. Our impatience makes us give up too quickly. However, speaking from experience, I can assure you that living this abundant life is well worth the work and sacrifice it will take. I'll explain the principles in detail and give you plenty of examples to help you to see what needs to be done. I promise it is worth the effort to gain freedom from the slavery of a besetting sin.

3. Sometimes Christians do not want to face life without that certain sin which seems so necessary and satisfying. We might not want to admit it, but sin can be enjoyable. In Hebrews 11:24–26, we read: "By faith Moses, ...choosing rather to endure ill-treatment with the people of God than to enjoy the passing pleasures of sin, considering the reproach of Christ greater riches than the treasures of Egypt; for he was looking to the reward." Moses chose the greater reward, but he had to push away the "passing pleasures" of sin. The addictions in our lives bring long-term pain, but they also bring short-term pleasures: sex outside marriage, mood altering drugs, the buzz from alcohol, or eating your favorite desert until you can't eat another bite. The list can go on indefinitely.

How I Figured This Out

When I became a Christian over 40 years ago, I was not looking for an abundant life. I had no idea it existed. I was just looking for a way to miss the judgment of God and avoid eternal punishment in hell. When I first trusted Christ, I had no Bible knowledge. If I listened to someone teach from the Bible, I was lost. I did not know how to find my way through all the books and verses.

As time went by, I was blessed to meet some Christians who were experiencing the abundant life Christ described. They were so full of joy and peace even though they had hard circumstances in life. They had clear direction and purpose in life, while so many of my peers and I were floundering in apathy and discontentment. They had the same temptations I had, but they seemed to have a supernatural ability to overcome. As I considered my life and theirs, it became obvious that theirs was significantly better. So, I decided to spend time with them and learn their secrets.

Much of this book is a direct result of spending time with them, talking to them, and imitating them. They pointed me to God and to a better way of living. These Christian friends became my mentors. They did not consider themselves as experts on living; they merely considered themselves fellow learners as they helped me. They taught me to depend on Christ. Their philosophy was to teach me to go the Bible and to find strength from God. And as I studied God's truths in the Bible, I, little-by-little, became a keen observer of human nature and a more objective student of my own life. I learned not to compare myself with people around me, but with the godly characters in the scriptures. I sought to emulate their thinking, lifestyles and values in everyday life.

Finally, after many years I realized that the Christian life isn't so much about doing but about being…. Being close to God, being loyal to Him, being a man of God who practices righteousness to bring God joy, being a man who genuinely cares about others and demonstrates it, and being a man who loves God supremely.

In the next chapter, I'll talk about our common struggle.

For a free video summary of this chapter by the author go online to www.dirtysecretsdirtylies.com and click on Free Videos.

2

Your Struggle and Mine

I'm Just Like You

At this point you are probably thinking, "Traylor, you don't have a clue what I'm really like. You have never had hang-ups even close to mine." Well, let me assure you that I have struggled and failed just like anyone else. I remember the days before I first trusted Christ. Lying, profanity, immorality, and substance abuse were all a significant part of my lifestyle. I can remember dozens of occasions which I promised God that I would change my ways, but I never had the power to do anything about it. I simply become more entrenched in the same bad habits. I was literally a slave to all of the bad character mentioned above in addition to several others. I was even a thief. I know now that had it not been for Christ changing my life, I would have ultimately ended up in prison somewhere for a very long time.

11

My bad moral choices left me emotionally empty and broken. My self-esteem was extremely low, and my relationships with others were sadly dysfunctional. My poor choices made people want to avoid me, which only increased my feelings of rejection and discouragement. Then, one day I got to start over.

Aha! Others Have Overcome and I Could, Too

I suppose I had heard the Gospel of Christ before, but that day—things were different. For the first time, I understood that there was a solution to MY problems, to my sin problem. It is dangerous to use the word "sin" because it sounds like a preachy evangelist on TV, but bear with me. Sin has two elements. It is a twisting, a corrupting, or a destruction of God's good plans for our lives, and it is an indifferent, rebellion toward God. Sin is pushing God out of our lives and thinking that we can create good lives without Him.

I had known for a long time that I was a sinner. No one had to convince me of that. What I did not realize until then was that Christ had already made a way to wash away the guilt I felt about my destructive thoughts and behaviors. Also, Jesus had already made a way to remove the guilt of my sins and I could be justified. This word means that God will forgive us and make our lives right, if we humbly accept Christ's payment on the cross for our sins. Understanding this key component to salvation will help us understand why we can have a right relationship with God. There are many things about God we don't understand, but it is clear in the Bible that God wants to forgive our sins, and He wants to give us a new strength to live successfully. What I am really talking about here is another Bible concept called "grace." Maybe you are like me, you've heard these Bible terms before, but you really were not sure what they mean. Grace is that quality in God's heart which wants to give His unconditional love to us and wants to give us strength for abundant living. Love is the very core of His being. However, there is another quality in God's heart: justice. Just as He wants the best for us, He hates the corruption, confusion, and destruction caused by sin. He hates the way people destroy others or destroy themselves. That's just the way He is. These two attributes came into direct opposition in our case. On the one hand, He sincerely loves us, but on the other hand we continually violate His plans, and we continually bring confusion and suffering into the lives of His creatures including ourselves. To judge rightly He was compelled to condemn us, but His unconditional commitment to us compelled Him to send His Son, Jesus Christ, to die and to pay for our sins.

Most of my life I had heard that Christ died on the cross for our sins, but somehow I never listened. That fact was too impersonal. It was too theoretical for me; it was just a big-picture concept. But one Friday night in March of 1971, I realized that I could be personally forgiven by God. That night, I personally put my faith in Christ and the payment He made for ME on the cross. I experienced real forgiveness and a peace which I had never had before. That was a great experience, but it wasn't until later that I understood that He also provided all the power that I needed to resist any temptation that life brought my way.

God helped me understand that He had washed away the guilt of my sins. That weekend in the March of 1971, He also had me meet some very special people. They were overcomers. They were saints of God in the true sense of saints. I did not really know them well, but they were people who were living holy and genuine lives. They were guests at the church I was attending. They were just there for the weekend, sharing the good news of God's forgiveness through Christ. Somehow I knew instinctively that these people were experiencing a walk with God and had supernatural power that I wanted. I wanted the new life that they were experiencing. I just knew that God would help me have it, too.

At that time, I prayed that God would send some mature, committed Christians into my life to teach me how to live successfully. Within a

For a free video summary of this chapter by the author go online to www.dirtysecretsdirtylies.com and click on Free Videos.

3

Overcoming Your Besetting Sin is a Process

Identify the Problem

Jared was broke again. He had a great job, but never had any money. Another time came: he had been cleaned out again at the Last Chance Casino. He was kicking himself. He was trying to come up with a new excuse to give his wife, Jennifer, about where their payday had gone. He knew she would rant and rave at him. He had tried so many times to stop gambling. He made new years' resolutions. He cried about it, prayed about it, and even promised Jennifer that he would never do it again …. Yet, also thought to himself, "Next time, I'll win." Each time, after the grief of loss and the shame and guilt subsided, he was back to his same habits and thought patterns. "This time it will be different. I'll play poker and I'll win. I've won in the past and I can do it again. I'll know when to stop after I win and I won't play anymore."

Inevitably the same results always happened. Either he would lose it all quickly or he would win and continue to play until his luck ran out and he lost it all.

This time he remembered something his buddy, Kevin always said, "The definition of insanity is doing the same thing over and over again, expecting different results." Jared thought, "Maybe that's the problem." He had trusted Kevin's advice before; maybe Kevin could help him this time. So, they talked. Kevin patiently listened to Jason even though he had heard Jason's story before. Kevin then suggested that maybe the problem is not the way he was playing, but what he was thinking. Kevin asked Jared what the casino was like. Jared said it was a very luxurious place. It was newly decorated, new furnishings and a lot of very friendly servers. The meals were great and very inexpensive. Then Kevin asked Jared, "How do you think the casino can afford to pay so much for that wonderful environment?" This was the first time Jared had ever thought about that. He said, "They must be winning a lot of money to furnish a place like that." Kevin agreed. For the first time Jared realized that losing at the casino is normal—thousands of people pass through and lose lots of money. He had been tricked into thinking that he could be a long-term winner playing against "the house." Kevin explained that the house always has the advantage. The odds are stacked in its favor, and the house has the resources to outlast the player.

There are many ways to identifying a besetting sin. Just as Jared in the story above had to come to grips with his problem, we must all accept that we have a problem. Chapter Four explores how observing our emotions and destructive behavior identifies the sin. Then, by tracing back our sin from our negative emotions and the destructive results, we realize our wrong actions. These actions guide us into our true motivation.

Find Your Source of Power

Continuing our story of Jared, he told Jennifer that he had once again lost his paycheck and about his eye opening conversation with Kevin. Jennifer was sick that he had lost the money, but actually she was kind of encouraged that Jared might be facing his problem. She also told him that she had been praying that God would reveal to him that gambling is a loser's game. It seems that God was getting through to Jared. In the end, Jennifer forgave him but warned him that old habits are hard to break and that he would be faced with the temptation to gamble his paycheck again. Jared initially said that he would never be tempted again to gamble since it was so obvious to him that gambling is a losing proposition.

The weeks went by and times were really tough for Jared, Jennifer and their family. Jared didn't have the money he needed to pay the house payment, so he borrowed the money to pay the note on his credit card. About that time he was feeling pretty down about his financial situation. The next day, Steve, one of his co-workers came to work all smiles and excited. He proudly announced that he had won $5,100 playing the slots at the Western Star Casino. Immediately, Jared thought, "If that idiot can win big, I can too." Suddenly he had this seemingly uncontrollable urge to go back to the Last Chance Casino and show everyone that he could be a winner too. He made up his mind that after work he would pull out some money on his credit card and try his luck. Right after work, he went straight to the cash machine and got the money. On his way over he was visualizing how he would go into the poker table and clean up. Suddenly, he remembered his conversations with Kevin and Jennifer. But the urge was so overwhelming. He realized for the first time that an intellectual agreement was not enough. He needed a supernatural power to resist the temptation. Suddenly he came face-to-face with his need for God to help him make the right choice. He thought, "How can something that feels so right be wrong?" There was a song that said that one time. With or without the song, people have tried to live according to those words. But, as the Bible says, sin does not give birth to real living; sin gives birth to self-destruction and death (see James 1:13–18).

In Chapter Five, we will see that it is impossible to change our attitudes and actions without finding God's source of power. Once the sin problem is identified, overcoming it is a process which takes time. Most people don't realize this. Too often we want instant success, but a besetting sin took hold of us over a period of time, and often it takes a long time to gain victory. But, there is hope. Thousands of people have appealed to God for strength and eventually, they conquered that nagging sin.

Search Out the Truth

Fortunately, as Jared felt those tempting thoughts build up like a thunderhead rain cloud, he asked the Lord to help him. And, God was gracious. He did not make the same foolish mistake that he had made so many times over the last 13 years. He left the casino parking lot without going inside. He decided to go to a quiet place to pray and carefully consider what was happening inside his heart. Even though his emotions were still raging within him, once he left the casino he started to calm down. His racing pulse slowed down and he started to think clearly again. How could he let his emotions so violently overpower him? How could he throw reason and logic out the window on such a whim? What could he do next time that would make it easier for him to resist?

In Chapter Six, we will study how to search out the truth in every besetting sin and how to incorporate the truth into your everyday experience to overcome whatever obstacle which blocks your success. This chapter will help you identify the lies you are that believing and empower you with the truth.

Act on What You Know is True

As he left the parking lot of the casino that day, the Lord reminded Jared that gambling is a losing proposition. Jared realized that once the strong desire to gamble came over him, it was nearly impossible for him to resist. The Lord showed him that he needed to be prepared for the next temptation, and that he needed to daily be proactive to resist the temptation.

In Chapter Seven we will cover the principle of preparation for warfare and the use of our will to not only resist temptation, but to build powerful, positive habits which will completely replace the grim hold which a besetting sin can have on our lives. Once the truth is understood, it must be integrated into our hearts and our will.

Solidify Your Faith and Emotions with Action

Over the next few months, although Jared had serious gambling struggles and some failures he became consistent in overcoming his gambling addiction. His faith was growing stronger day-by-day, week-by-week, as he allowed his faith instead of his emotions to control his actions. At first the struggle to stop gambling was an almost overwhelming pull. At times everything within him screamed to go to the poker table. Through consistently reminding himself of the truth about gambling and exercising his will even when he didn't feel like it, he noticed his emotions were changing. He consistently found that he was happier, more peaceful, more content and even more satisfied. Since he had stopped gambling, he and Jennifer actually had money to start paying off their credit card debt. As time went by they even had extra money. Suddenly they had options. They were gaining freedom from gambling and debt, and they were gaining freedom to enjoy life together.

In Chapter Eight, we will discuss how faith and actions impact emotions. We will explore how to consistently have joy, no matter what circumstances we are facing. Additionally, we will look at how to reverse the negative emotions of anger, wrath, malice, shame, anxiety and guilt.

Substitute the Positive for Negative

No longer financially strapped by Jared's gambling addictions, Jared and Jennifer found they had new financial options. One Sunday a visiting missionary was the guest speaker at church. Both Jared and Jennifer had always felt a yearning in their hearts to give whenever a missionary couple spoke. Often at church, the missionaries would show pictures of very poor people and outrageous living conditions in other parts of the world. People needed clean water wells for their villages or medical clinics for the malnourished children. Jared and Jennifer always went home and shut the images out of their consciousness because they were not in any financial place to give. Now things were different. They had extra money that Sunday when the representatives from Compassion International showed the slides. They didn't make a rash decision that day, but after a week of prayer and discussion they decided to sponsor a child. They felt they could commit to that and decided to go for it. Over the months they began to get to know the little boy through letters and photos. As time went by, God laid it on their heart the goal of sponsoring twenty children. They suddenly knew that what they were making was not enough if they were going to successfully reach their goal. Jared prayed about it and within a short time God gave him an opportunity to move on to a different company with a promotion. Once again, God was faithful, and they were able to give abundantly. They had learned to substitute the positive thoughts and actions for the negative, believing God to supply all their needs.

In Chapter Nine, we will remove the myth that the Christian life is a list of things not to do. The Christian life is positive; it is really about loving God and using His power to embrace the good that God has for us to experience and to do. We will learn practical steps that can transform our negative destructive thoughts and actions into a positive, powerful, fulfilling life with fantastic ramifications.

Accountability—Pursue Righteousness, and Other Things with those who call on the Lord from a Pure Heart

There is one thing that I haven't mentioned in the story about Jared and Jennifer. They developed a close relationship with two members of their church: Kevin and his wife Betsy. These two couples were part of a closely knit small support group at their church. The members of the support group were genuine believers in the Lord Jesus Christ. They not only had a strong commitment to Christ; they really loved one another. When one member of the group was hurting, they all hurt. When one was excited about something, they all rejoiced. Their lives were really intertwined for the good of one another. Without the support which Jared and Jennifer received, Jared probably would have slipped back into his gambling addiction, and Jennifer would have reverted back to the negative, nagging wife she was before. The group consistently reached outside itself to minister to the needs of others. They regularly went together down to the Salvation Army to help in the food pantry and sometimes they helped less fortunate children in the AWANAS program.

In Chapter Ten you'll learn that a support group is essential in staying strong in Christ. We will explore examples of small groups in the Bible and in today's culture. This is a very important chapter, so you'll want to spend time working through it. I'll give some practical tips on how to thrive in a small group.

Visualize the End from the Beginning

Jared and Jennifer's story is pretty consistent in the way most Christians learn to overcome their besetting sins. They, and many Christians, could have done something which would have made the process much easier. They should have sought to gain God's perspective about their lives from the very beginning of their journey over their besetting sin. We forget that God can see the "big picture" of our whole lives. God can see the abilities and maturity which we will eventually gain after we go through the process of His training. If we could see into the future and see the end result of our struggles, then we would more readily overcome our difficulties today. But God does see the end. He knows where our path is leading, and He is always there setting things in motion to accomplish the end result. If Jared had seen the end result of his life as a giver and provider for underprivileged children in third world countries, he would have had a reason to leave gambling far behind. He would have been motivated to excel at his job and earn the promotion sooner. It would have brought him and Jennifer to a place of joy, contentment and personal satisfaction much sooner.

In Chapter Eleven we will learn to visualize the end or goal of our lives. This will help us take the steps we need to take so we will be transformed into the image of Christ and to be useful to Him in everything we do. This powerful biblical concept will radically accelerate our progress and give us the courage and confidence we need to become all that God intended.

Biggest Obstacles

After reading the preceding paragraphs, it might seem that I believe it is simple and easy to overcome besetting sins. Let me set the record straight. Overcoming besetting sins is a process which takes time. The biggest obstacle you or anyone will face is believing that you can overcome that nagging sin. There are two other major obstacles which might hinder us. We might not find mentors to help guide us, or we might not find a big enough reason "why" we should fight and overcome our besetting sins.

In Chapter Twelve, we will be able to learn about these two obstacles and discuss ways to overcome them. We need practical instruction about where to find help and what to do when things really look bleak and hopeless.

Others Succeeded, You Can, Too

In Chapter Thirteen, we will investigate how we can have a framework for success. We will look at examples of men and women with besetting sins who were victorious. These examples will reinforce the truth that we too can have victory as we lay aside the old habits and proactively pursue righteousness and godliness. You won't want to miss the inspiring stories of victory. And yes, there are even stories of those who lacked faith and allowed sin to rule them. Both are testimonies of the faithfulness of God and ramifications of not taking hold of God's promises. Finally, we need the hope that as we implement some very practical steps, we can take hold of all that God has for us.

Look What's Coming

Looking ahead we are excited to know that we do not need to be slaves to our old addictions. Usually, we don't even realize we have a problem until it has caused widespread destruction in our lives and in the lives of our loved ones. In the next chapter, we will look at some practical insights into how to quickly identify our issues so we can get the help we need.

For a free video summary of this chapter by the author go online to www.dirtysecretsdirtylies.com and click on Free Videos.

4

Identify the Problem

What's Really Wrong with Me

Josh and Brittney married seven years ago. Like most newlyweds, they dreamed about starting a family. Before long, Micah was born. He is now six years old. He is wonderful, healthy, and full of life. They love him so much, but they are starting to realize that he is a selfish little brat. His favorite word is "NO!" He will not share his toys, and he never goes to bed without pitching a royal fit. Sound familiar? You know the drill. Brittney is very concerned about Micah. The more she tried to correct him, the madder he got. Why did they have to teach him to be good; bad behavior seemed so automatic. Something was inherently wrong here. Modern psychologists call him maladjusted or maladapted.

Interesting enough, the Bible has a very clear and different explanation of the state of humanity. The Bible paints a portrait of mankind being spiritually dead. It states that humans are constantly resisting and rebelling against God. In the following passages I will piece together the series of events which bought us to this condition. We go back to how it all began in the Garden of Eden:

> The LORD God commanded the man, saying, "From any tree of the garden you may eat freely; but from the tree of the knowledge of good and evil you shall not eat, for in the day that you eat from it you will surely die."
>
> **Genesis 2:16–17**

At first glance, it appears that God meant immediate physical death would occur when they ate of the fruit of the knowledge of good and evil. Well, things did not play out that way exactly. In the next chapter, temptation reared it appealing head, and Eve fell for it.

> Now the serpent was more crafty than any beast of the field which the LORD God had made. And he said to the woman, "Indeed, has God said, 'You shall not eat from any tree of the garden'?" The woman said to the serpent, "From the fruit of the trees of the garden we may eat; but from the fruit of the tree which is in the middle of the garden, God has said, 'You shall not eat from it or touch it, or you will die.'" The serpent said to the woman, "You surely will not die. "For God knows that in the day you eat from it your eyes will be opened, and you will be like God, knowing good and evil." When the woman saw that the tree was good for food, and that it was a delight to the eyes, and that the tree was desirable to make one wise, she took from its fruit and ate; and she gave also to her husband with her, and he ate. Then the eyes of both of them were opened, and they knew that

they were naked; and they sewed fig leaves together and
made themselves loin coverings.

Genesis 3:1–7

Clearly, Adam and Eve ate the fruit of the tree of the knowledge
of good and evil, and they did not physically die. So, was God wrong
about the outcome or did we just misunderstand what He meant? I
think the answer is we just didn't understand what He was saying back
in Genesis chapter two. If we move to the New Testament, we find a
fuller explanation. We will look at what both Jesus and the Apostle Paul
said about our sin problem.

Jesus gives the first direct clue to the meaning of Genesis 3:1–7. In
his famous discussion with Nicodemus, we read:

Jesus answered and said to him, "Truly, truly, I say to you,
unless one is born again he cannot see the kingdom of God."
Nicodemus said to Him, "How can a man be born when
he is old? He cannot enter a second time into his mother's
womb and be born, can he?" Jesus answered, "Truly, truly,
I say to you, unless one is born of water and the Spirit he
cannot enter into the kingdom of God.

John 3:3–5

The passage is well-known and frequently quoted. Entire books have
been written about being born again. Since 21st century Christians are so
familiar with this passage, it is easy to think that Nicodemus and others
at time would have clearly understood this phrase: "born again". But
at that time, this concept was unknown to everyone. Reading through
the passage reveals that Nicodemus did not understand what Jesus was
talking about. His reaction shows how bazaar the concept was to him.
He asked Jesus, "How can a man enter back into his mother's womb and

be born again?" Jesus was referring to a restoration of the spiritual life of the believer which was lost in the Garden account of Genesis 3:1–7.

Later, the Apostle Paul points out the basic, original condition of humans in numerous passages. For example, in Ephesians 2:1–5 we read:

> And you were dead in your trespasses and sins, in which you formerly walked according to the course of this world, according to the prince of the power of the air, of the spirit that is now working in the sons of disobedience. Among them we too all formerly lived in the lusts of our flesh, indulging the desires of the flesh and of the mind, and were by nature children of wrath, even as the rest. But God, being rich in mercy, because of His great love with which He loved us, even when we were dead in our transgressions, made us alive together with Christ (by grace you have been saved),

In this familiar New Testament passage, Paul makes some clear and undeniable claims about the state of mankind without Christ. In verse 1, he calls us dead in trespasses and sins. We are dead to God without Christ. This certainly shows we need to be "born again" to God—as Jesus said to Nicodemus. Finally, in verse five, the apostle states that believers have been made alive (same as born again) together with Christ.

There are many other passages which also discuss this spiritual deadness. In other places, it is described as being alienated to God, without hope in the world, hostile to God, and being children of wrath. These are not pleasant images of our state without Christ, but they obviously explain why we are naturally bent toward evil and have such a hard time being good. One thing that modern psychologists and neurologists have been recently reporting is that these behavioral issues are a "hard wired" part of our existence. I'll give you more information about that in the addictions part which follows.

Addictions May be Harder Than You Think

The Scriptures continually discusses the two big areas of temptation. They are "the world" and "the flesh." We need to study what these two terms mean. The devil, or Satan, is the master manipulator of these two types of temptation. He uses deceptive suggestions to entice us to follow his suggestions which only wreak havoc in our lives.

In this section, we will explore fleshly addictions. In the next section, we will review the temptations of the world. Of course, these two are intricately intertwined and usually difficult to see independently.

As stated in the precious section, the fall of mankind ended our natural relationship to God. We died to God and became alive to sin. In our new natural state, we became slaves of sin, without the ability to consistently resist it. To study more on this subject, a thorough study of Romans chapters 1–8 is in order. There are many books available to help you better understand this important part of the Bible. If you haven't studied it in detail, that would be very worthwhile.

Since the late 15th century the word "addiction" has been batted around. Simply put addictions are destructive habits which cause trauma if they are discontinued. That really describes the flesh. Why are addictions so hard to deal with? In the next paragraph I give a short physiological explanation about why addictions are so hard to overcome.

Gerald May, MD wrote in his book, *Addiction and Grace*, that there are approximately 30 different neurotransmitter chemicals which are collected by billions of neuroreceptors primarily in the brain. These neurotransmitter chemicals are also connected to an intricate network of nerves throughout the body. Most of these chemicals are created to some degree naturally in our bodies, although some are injected into the system though the blood or digestive system. This interplay of neurological chemical reactions on brain cells, and they create the pathos or feelings of our lives. These chemicals are naturally created in our bodies for a variety of reasons. Actually, all of them are created completely unknown to us based on the body's functional needs such as to sleep, digest our food, pump our blood, etc. Other chemicals are naturally created based on perception by our brains for simple and complex needs and desires such as pain, pleasure and higher level responses such as sympathy, empathy, romance, loyalty as well as many other human factors too long to list. In addition to the chemicals produced naturally by the body, sometimes we artificially introduce these chemicals into our bodies either abusively or constructively to create a euphoric or healing effects. Whenever we artificially introduce these chemicals or stimulate the production of these chemicals excessively, it creates a dependence on the chemical which researchers commonly call the balance between equilibrium and stress. When an excessive amount of a euphoric chemical is introduced into the neurological system, the cell structure secretes less of the reactionary chemical which stimulates the cells to naturally create the chemical. This overabundance quickly becomes the new equilibrium. When the supply of the overabundant chemical is cut off, the receptor cells send signals to the producing cells to make more. This balance of equilibrium and stress is the basis for severe withdrawals from destructive chemicals such as narcotics and alcohol.

Obviously this is a very elementary explanation of the chemical processes which take place when alien chemicals are introduced into our neurological systems. Bear with me, because many of these same chemicals, which control our emotions, are produced naturally as we follow Christ. This new birth enables us to have the power to do the right things which stimulates a chemical creation process which then stimulates positive emotions.

The World–Satan's Playground

As I promised earlier, we need to explore the second area of temptation – the world. The world we have today is a completely different place from what God initially created. The Genesis account states that God's initial creation was good (see Genesis chapter one). He was pleased with it, and it was a utopian state. It was perfect in every way. When mankind sinned in Genesis chapter 3 as we noted earlier, humans started to experience spiritual death, and the entire of creation was corrupted. God cursed the earth and the entire eco-system was transformed.

> And I will put enmity between you and the woman, and between your seed and her seed; He shall bruise you on the head, And you shall bruise him on the heel." To the woman He said, "I will greatly multiply your pain in childbirth, in pain you will bring forth children; yet your desire will be for your husband, And he will rule over you." Then to Adam He said, "Because you have listened to the voice of your wife, and have eaten from the tree about which I commanded you, saying, 'You shall not eat from it'; Cursed is the ground because of you; In toil you will eat of it All the days of your life. "Both thorns and thistles it shall grow for you; And you will eat the plants of the field; By the sweat of your face You will eat bread, Till you return to the ground, Because from it you were taken; For you are dust, And to dust you shall return."
>
> **Gen 3:15–19**

> For we know that the whole creation groans and suffers the pains of childbirth together until now.
>
> **Rom 8:22**

At first God made the humans guardians of the earth. The entire eco-system worked harmoniously together, and it seem that the animals were friendly and co-operative—not adversarial. The garden was easily managed with natural watering systems and abundant fruitfulness.

However, sin brought a new world order which created tenseness and discord between humans and between humanity and the rest of creation. Several things happened. The land became less fertile compared to what it was in the Garden of Eden. Adversarial vegetation was introduced such as thorns and thistles. Work was much more difficult and stressful. In addition, all living creatures would eventually die.

Finally, there was a new master ruling over the earth. The earth became the domain of God's adversary, Satan, who is called "the Prince of the Power of the Air" (Ephesians 2:2). Satan and his demons sought to control and to enslave God's supreme creation, mankind. This new world order is the antithesis of the values of God wanted. All of God's attributes were set aside and high value was placed on the opposite attribute. Here are a few examples:

God's Attitude	Antithesis
Humility	Pride of Life-Comparisons/ Power
Service to Others	Selfishness
Giving	Taking: Lust of the Eyes- Greed/Covetous

We have all been born into this new hostile environment. Thanks be to God, that reflecting on the circumstances around us, we now have the ability to understand what our real problems are and a way to escape from the slavery of this environment.

Look for Symptoms

The way we identify our problems is by looking for symptoms. When we are sick we evaluate our symptoms. We usually don't know what is wrong, even though you may have a good idea. Sometimes it isn't easy to determine what is wrong even though we have symptoms. I'll give you an example.

When my son was about twelve, he fell from a tree and hurt his arm. We knew what hurt his arm… falling from the tree. The problem was we did not know the extent of the damage. Was it a sprain? Was it maybe a hairline fracture or a clear break? Fortunately, we realized that since we did not know how bad it really was, we took him to the doctor. The doctor did an x-ray and found a broken arm. He was in a cast for several weeks and he eventually recovered. I'm glad we went to the doctor and took care of the problem, because he can really play the piano and guitar now. Suppose that he had not experienced the pain which is a symptom of the break, we would never have taken him to the doctor. If we had not taken him for treatment, he probably would have experienced more damage to his arm as he continued to use it in it damaged state. God gave us pain (a symptom) so we would know to tend to a physical ailment. The same is true of emotional and spiritual pain. These, too, are symptoms which we need to recognize so we can find healing. If we don't realize we have a problem, we will not get the help we need to overcome the root problem.

Negative Emotions are Telling Signs

Most of us react to negative emotions by denying we have them. We might say, "No, I'm not mad.", but we are really fuming. Sometimes we agree with the negative emotions and say something like, "You think this is mad? I'll show you MAD!" Other times we react as victims, "Yes, I'm mad, but I can't do anything about it." Let us explore these issues a little.

Patrick was so angry at Amanda. He knew he needed to forgive her, but could not let go of his anger. He told himself, "She is so low that I don't ever want to speak to her again. I don't think I'll ever feel like forgiving her for what she has done to me." The next day he was still fuming. When he met up with his buddy, Troy, he verbally lit into Amanda. When he and Troy saw her walking across the street, Patrick said, "I can't stand her. Let's get out of here."

Does this sound familiar? How many times have you been around someone who reacted with a negative emotion like anger and allowed it to control him or her? Maybe you have even reacted that way. Allowing our emotions to control us is as old as the human race itself. In Genesis chapter four a similar emotional exchange ended in murder. Notice how God addresses the negative emotion and Cain's response to anger.

So it came about in the course of time that Cain brought an offering to the LORD of the fruit of the ground. Abel, on his part also brought of the firstlings of his flock and of their fat portions. And the LORD had regard for Abel and for his offering; but for Cain and for his offering He had no regard. So Cain became very angry and his countenance fell. Then the LORD said to Cain, "Why are you angry? And why has your countenance fallen? "If you do well, will not your countenance be lifted up? And if you do not do well, sin is crouching at the door; and its desire is for you, but you must master it." Cain told Abel his brother. And it came about when they were in the field, that Cain rose up against Abel his brother and killed him. Gen 4:3–8

This passage is foundational to understanding the source of emotions. The human race cannot exist without emotions. It is a normal part of our makeup. In the case of Patrick above, he allowed his emotions to control his actions. The same thing happen to Cain in the Genesis chapter four account above. Cain was angry with God because his sacrifice was unacceptable to God. He compared himself to his brother Able. It made him mad that Abel's sacrifice was acceptable to God. God sincerely cared about Cain, but that did not justify allowing him to have his own way. God wanted Cain to humble himself and accept His rules, but Cain remained prideful. God gives us some important insights into the human condition when he asked Cain why his countenance had fallen. His facial expression indicated his inner emotions. If Cain would do the right thing, then his emotions would be transformed. This interaction between doing the right thing and experiencing positive or negative emotions is directly related. If we do well (the right thing) our countenance (emotions) will be lifted up.

In Patrick's case above, doing the right thing was to forgive Amanda. However, Patrick was unwilling to do the right thing and forgive. As a result, he never got over his anger and resentment. He countenance was never lifted up. There is a long list of negative emotions. Becoming aware that you are experiencing some of them is important in identifying besetting sins. Some of the negative emotions include anger, bitterness, jealousy, strife, envy, shame, dehumanized, disrespected, humiliated, suppressed, manipulated, abandoned, confused, alone, disapproved of, discouraged, ignored, insignificance, invisible, blamed, cheated, accused, disbelieved, resentful, teased, ridiculed, interrogated, worthless, unloved, unwanted, abused, afraid, defensive, intimidated, cynical, suspicious and untrusting.

Trace the Root from Destructive or Harmful Behavior

Another way to realize a person has a besetting sin is to recognize destructive behavior he or she exhibits.

Emily had a hot temper. Whenever she had a bad day, you better watch out. She would start attacking anybody or anything. There is an old saying, "When Mama ain't happy, ain't nobody happy." Today is one of those days. Emily's boss is overwhelmed with pressures. As a result, Emily has extra work and extra pressure to keep everything humming along at the office. Even before the extra work, Emily had been feeling overwhelmed at work and home, now she was ready to explode. She could not complain to her boss and risk getting "fired" because her family needed that income to pay their bills. She did all the extra work, but she really resented it. By the time she got home, she wanted to explode emotionally. Now that she was home, she felt she had a right to throw a fit with her husband and kids. When she hit the door, she immediately saw that her husband, Tyler had not cleaned out the garage like he had promised and that her daughter, Kayla was not home yet from school. She immediately thought, "Those two expect me to do everything. Well, I'm going to let them know that I'm nobody's maid." When Tyler got home she immediately tore into him about the garage. She called him every name in the book and told him he better get out in the garage and straighten it or he could find somewhere else to spend the night. When Kayla got home around 8 PM, Emily let her have "both barrels". She called Kayla lazy, undisciplined, and hateful. She also told them both that she didn't think they cared about anything but themselves. This type of abusive speech is called "reviling" in the Bible. It is such a serious offense that the Apostle Paul recommended that people who practice reviling on a regular basis should be excommunicated from church fellowship (see I Corinthians 5:11).

The story about Emily is just one example of how our negative emotions can help us identify deeper, root problems. Earlier, we looked at a list of negative emotions. Those negative emotions lead to all kinds of destructive behavior. But underneath the emotions and before the destructive behavior, there was a besetting sin. The real challenge is peeling back the layers of emotions and destructive behavior so we can identify the wrong thoughts which are driving us. That's why I say overcoming besetting sins is a process which takes time, patience, and the grace of God.

Common Besetting Sins

Because we are so creative in our rebellion against God's plan for us, the possible list of besetting sins is very long. In fact, we will never have a complete list of them. With that said, here is a list which is a starting point for understanding this topic. Realize that some of these sins may spring from the same root.

Here is a partial list:

Malice	Slander	Anger outbursts
Abusive speech	Idolatry	Impurity
Sensuality	Greed	Stinginess
Blasphemy	Profanity	Sorcery
Gluttony	Lustful passion	Sexual immorality
Pornography	Stealing	Coveting
Swindling	Lying	Cheating
Reviling	Abusing alcohol	Disputing
Dissenting	and drugs	Gossiping
Quarreling	Divisive	Murdering
Flattering	Carousing	
False Teaching		

Don't Get Discouraged

I realize that this chapter can be discouraging, because it faces our weakness head-on. The first step to any solution is recognizing a problem exists. At this point I want to encourage you. The first step in identifying the problem is to ask God for wisdom in coming to understand exactly what is wrong. The next step is to go to God because He has the solution to whatever we are facing. And, God has abundant resources to get us through those problems. In the next chapter, we will look at God's remarkable power—in particular, we will look at the person of the Holy Spirit who will lead us to triumph.

For a free video summary of this chapter by the author go online to www.dirtysecretsdirtylies.com and click on Free Videos.

5

Find Your
Source of Power

What You Need In Order to Get the Power

Everyone wants the power to live life to the fullest. Problem is we don't always pursue the abundant life which Christ promotes. Sometimes we think we are going down the right path when really the end result is far from the best for ourselves or others. In the previous chapter, I explained there is an inherent problem with human existence. We live in a fallen world with fallen people who are not usually pursuing God's best for their lives and others. Lisa was an example of that.

Lisa was a favorite of all the football players in high school. She liked all the attention they gave her, but really didn't take any of the guys too seriously. She just liked to flirt with them all and keep them all wishing. It was a way to stroke her huge ego. Joey was a shy, introverted team member who was really nervous around girls. Lisa liked to see how many of the guys she could attract. Joey never had an attractive girl pay him any attention, but Lisa flirted with and flattered him just like she did everyone. Whenever Joey was around Lisa, he was completely drawn to her. Problem was, he thought Lisa was really interested in him. Over the short football season, Joey was completely tricked by her flirtations. He saw her flirting with other guys, and that bothered him, yet she always made him feel so special. He quickly became infatuated with her. He went back and forth in his mind and finally decided to ask Lisa to be his date to the homecoming dance. He was so afraid to ask her out that he waited until a week before the dance. When he finally got up the courage, three other guys had already asked her out. She wasn't willing to give an answer to any of them, even though she had already made her selection. Like I said, she loved the attention. Every day that went by each guy asked her again. She loved it. With only two days left, she finally told Jerry that he would be her date. Joey was crushed. He really thought that Lisa cared about him.

Flattery is a form of deception which compliments a person insincerely in order to gain an advantage. Lisa was a master of this kind of deception. We can't completely blame Lisa for it. She was an understudy of her mom, who taught her everything she knew about deception. Of course her mom was not the originator or deception. Therein lies the problem. We live in a fallen world which is shrouded in deceit. We are even born into this existence completely unaware that it is broken. By saying broken, I mean far from what God intended or intends today. Idealistic as we may be, we find that we are held captive by our own selfish impulses and lusts completely unable to consistently overcome the most basic character deficiencies such as lying, cheating, stealing, and many others too numerous to list here. No wonder we have such a hard time even recognizing there is a problem.

So how do we break out of this miserable existence of slavery to sin? The first step in this process is to experience the new spiritual birth

I alluded to in the last chapter. In this chapter I will expand on this concept and give you hope that you can break the cycle of enslavement to your own personal sin and become effective in equipping others to be overcomers.

As I discussed in the last chapter, Jesus gives the first indication that we can be spiritually born again in His famous statements in John chapter three which were quoted earlier. Peter alludes to same experience in his first letter recorded in the Bible.

> Blessed be the God and Father of our Lord Jesus Christ, who according to His great mercy has caused us to be born again to a living hope through the resurrection of Jesus Christ from the dead, to obtain an inheritance which is imperishable and undefiled and will not fade away, reserved in heaven for you, who are protected by the power of God through faith for a salvation ready to be revealed in the last time.
>
> **1 Peter 1:3–5**

In this passage, Peter makes it clear that God transforms people by giving them a spiritual rebirth. This new spiritual life brings hope: both a hope of eternal life in the future and a hope of God's love and guidance today. This new birth is supernatural. It is a gift from God.

> As Moses lifted up the serpent in the wilderness, even so must the Son of Man be lifted up; so that whoever believes will in Him have eternal life. "For God so loved the world, that He gave His only begotten Son, that whoever believes in Him shall not perish, but have eternal life.
>
> **John 3:14–16**

Believing in Christ and gaining eternal life is the starting point for all of us. At this point I need to ask you a personal question. Have you personally put your faith in Christ and His payment for your sins? Unless you have done this there is no hope for you. As Jesus said in John 3:7b, "... you must be born again!" If you have never done this, I urge you now to set this book aside and admit your sins and tell Christ that you believe in Him and His promise of eternal life. Let Him know that you are willing to follow His plan throughout the rest of your life. If you do that, God is faithful to keep his side of the bargain. He will grant you an abundant and eternal life. He wants to give all of us deep and rich lives – more than we could ever dream was possible. I'm so glad I did that over forty years ago. It is the best step I have ever taken.

This First Step is Only the Beginning

The entire Christian life is a relationship of trust in God; it is listening to God's truths in the Bible and acting and thinking in new ways. In the Bible, it says,

> "Therefore, as you received Christ Jesus the Lord, so walk in Him."
>
> Colossians 2:6

So what will happen if you are a new believer in Christ? I can tell you from firsthand experience that you are in for a wonderful life which starts in faith and continues to grow through faith. This life of faith is a trusting relationship with God. We will face challenges, but it will be exhilarating and fulfilling. We will face stresses, but with every challenge we will have opportunities to see God keep His promises and we will learn to walk, step-by-step with the Creator of the universe.

Victory that Overcomes the World, Our Faith

> Whoever believes that Jesus is the Christ is born of God, and whoever loves the Father loves the child born of Him. By this we know that we love the children of God, when we love God and observe His commandments. For this is the love of God, that we keep His commandments; and His commandments are not burdensome. For whatever is born of God overcomes the world; and this is the victory that has overcome the world—our faith.
>
> 1John 5:1–4

These concepts are easy to grasp but their implications are often hard to put into practice. If you have ever tried to consistently do the right thing, you know what I am talking about. In your head you know what you are doing is wrong. You even want to lay it aside, but it is beyond your grasp to turn away from it. Finding freedom from our sins takes a supernatural power which we don't have. From the passage above, it's clear that any victory we have in overcoming the world and our flesh is linked to our faith in Christ and His promises. As a believer in Christ, we have a new and sincere love for God and the desire to please Him. It is a God-given desire which resonates throughout our being. From the beginning of our new spiritual life we long to keep His commandments in order to demonstrate our love for Him.

What if I Have a Crisis in My Faith?

However, just because we believe in Christ and we have gained eternal life that does not mean that we will always do the right thing.

Philip was a new believer. Like many before him, he was excited about his new relationship with God. He was "gung-ho." He felt bulletproof. After six months of having faith in Jesus and learning to walk with God, he had seen many victories. He broke ties with his old drinking buddies, and he even broke off his immoral relationship with Ashley, his girlfriend of three years. That was really tough, but the Lord was with him and brought him through. His new faith had brought him into contact with many other believers in his church.

One day, Philip and Jody, a friend from church, were sharing Christ with Scott, a guy from Philip's job. After they finished, Jody became very critical of how Philip was relating to Scott. Jody was very discouraging to Philip and it really took a toll on Philip.

Philip had already been discouraged about how he had handled his breakup with Ashley. He wondered if maybe he was doing more harm than good. In the days which followed, Philip took a more inward approach to life, re-examining his motives and actions. Philip started to think, "Who am I to be preaching to these people?" At that point, Philip pulled back from the Lord.

For the first time since trusting Christ, he felt alone and rejected. These feelings seemed to overwhelm him. Within days he was back to many of his old habits. For the first time since being born again, He picked up a six-pack of beer and began to forget his troubles. The next three weeks were a blur to Philip. It seemed that he was making one bad choice after another.

By now he was in full blown depression. He felt worthless and unworthy of ever approaching God since he had failed Him so miserably. Eric, Philip's friend, was there when Philip first came to Christ. After about a month, Eric realized something must have happened to Philip since he was not coming to church anymore. After work one evening, Eric stopped by to see Philip. Philip was very defensive. Eric could see through that defensiveness, and realized that Philip was very discouraged.

What Do You Do When You Don't Do the Right Things?

Fortunately Eric was there for Philip. Sadly, that is not always the case. More than once, King David of Old Testament went through a time of crisis in his faith. Sometimes he had a friend to help him, such as Jonathan. And, sometimes he had to go through the crises alone. Early in David's life, when he was still a teenager, God came through for him in a great way. He went up into battle against Goliath, the hero of the Philistines. I will not go into the details about the battle because you are probably very familiar with it. In one short skirmish David slew his nemesis and became the most celebrated warrior in all Israel. Not only did he get hero status, he got to marry the King Saul's daughter. He was also put in charge of the armies of Israel. His good fortune continued and the Lord brought him victory after victory to the extent that his fame grew to rival and to exceed that of the king, himself. Sounds like a storybook ending.

Through a series of struggles, David proved to be righteous and eventually became King of Israel after Saul was slain in battle. David started out this saga as the humble servant of the Lord. By the time we get to chapter 11 of 2nd Samuel, David had changed. It's not really clear why, but he neglected his duty as king and commander of the army. He sent others to go fight the nation's battles and he stayed home to enjoy the good life. As the story unfolded, he did like most men of power, he took certain liberties which he had no right to take. In the infamous story of David and Bathsheba, David committed adultery and his life was forever damaged.

After this sin, he tried to deceive Uriah, the husband of Bathsheba. When that manipulation failed, David plotted to have Uriah killed in the heat of battle to cover up his wrong. Sadly, this story (which you should read in the Bible) is a perfect example of the subject of this book. His adultery with Bathsheba was a dirty secret, which led to dirty lies and deceptive actions. This progression of events brought a curse from God on David and his family. Although David was ultimately forgiven by God for his sins, he still suffered a great deal for his actions.

David's sins devastated his family and the people of Israel lost their trust in him. Later, one of his sons lead an army of men to try to kill David, and much of the nation rejected David – at least for a period of time. Things would have been even worse, if it had not been for Nathan, a genuine friend of David, who confronted him and guided him back to God.

David's Restoration

...How blessed is he whose transgression is forgiven, whose sin is covered. How blessed is the man to whom the LORD does not impute iniquity, and in whose spirit there is no deceit. When I kept silent about my sin, my body wasted away through my groaning all day long. For day and night your hand was heavy upon me; My vitality was drained away as with the fever heat of summer. Selah. I acknowledged my sin to You, and my iniquity I did not hide; I said, "I will confess my transgressions to the LORD"; And You forgave the guilt of my sin. Selah.

Psalms 32:1–5

In this passage, David gives us a model of how we should act, think, and pray, if we stumble and fall back into our besetting sin. The first two verses exclaim the exhilarating emotions which come from following this cleansing process. But, before we can feel that joy and freedom of forgiveness, we need to follow the steps which David followed.

First Things First

First, we need to be honest with ourselves and with God. It is natural and normal to cover up our wrong doings. We have all done it. We do not want to get into any more trouble, so we just deny the wrong doing. That is exactly what David had been doing about his sin with Bathsheba and Uriah. The emotional and physical results of this cover up were obvious. Look at a list of things that happened to David when he was not honest:

"...body wasted away"— Sick, weak and impotent.

"...groanings all day long"—Emotionally experiencing the blues?

"...day and night Your hand was heavy upon me. —Constant guilt and shame and feelings of oppression.

"...my vitality was drained away"—Lifeless, not motivated, discouraged, hopeless.

I Will

Somehow, David recognized his situation and chose to do something about it. Nathan's confrontation with David possibly helped him remember what to do. He said,

"I acknowledged my sin to you"—He admitted his guilt and stopped the deception. "My iniquity I did not hide"—He stopped trying to cover up the sin and the embarrassment. He confessed the sin to God and others.

"I will confess my transgressions to the Lord, and You will forgive the guilt of my sin."—He chose to humbly come to God. He claimed God's promises of forgiveness and love.

Encouragement to Others in the Same Position

In Psalm 32, we read, "Let everyone who is godly pray to you in a time when you may be found." Here, David is realizing that this forgiveness and restoration is available to anyone who is willing to lay aside deceit, confess wrong doing, and turn to the Lord. Is there anything in your life you have habitually covered up? Do you believe that God will forgive you? I urge you to be honest with yourself and with God so you can experience the forgiveness and cleansing that will start you on the path to abundant living. If you do that, you will experience the thrill of restoration and new hope for the future.

Now to Him Who is Able to do Exceeding Abundantly Beyond All We Ask or Think—Ephesians 3:20a

When our negative emotions get overloaded, sometimes we don't believe we can do anything productive. Like David in the previous passage, we can be so discouraged about our failings that we do not even want to try anymore. In the passage from Ephesians 3 above, it does not say that God can do great things, if we feel like He can. Our feelings have nothing to do with it. God is able to do much more than what we ask or think, whether we feel like, or even believe, that He can.

Sometimes the job God has given us is really too difficult for us. If you've been a Christian very long, you know that God asks us to do things which are out of our comfort zone. Actually, they are really impossible unless we learn to trust in His supernatural help.

Paul, the Apostle, Who was a Mere Mortal

When we read about the characters in the Bible, it is amazing how human and weak they are. Sometimes we admire the people in the Bible so much that we overlook their weaknesses, their failures, and their sins.

They struggled just like we do today. Paul is one of my favorite Bible characters, not only because He was mightily used by God, but because his humanity gives me hope. He often mentions his frailties in his letters.

> I was with you in weakness and in fear and in much trembling.
>
> **1 Corinthians 2:3**

I can relate to that. It seems that I experience that regularly. Just today, I woke up almost in panic mode. Over the past few months I believe God has been leading me in several things which are really beyond my abilities. I felt sick at my stomach, fear made my heart race, and anxiety plagued my thoughts. "What if I tried and failed?" "What would people think and say?" "Why am I trying to do things which are so beyond me?" "Don't you have a lick of sense?" All these thoughts were racing through my mind. They stirred up a well of negative emotions which were almost paralyzing.

> Then I was reminded by the Lord, "… my grace is sufficient for you, for my power is perfected in weakness."
>
> **2 Corinthians 12:9a**

I said to the Lord, "Your power is available to me to accomplish all those things which you lay on my heart." Over the course of the morning, the negative emotions were replaced by the joy and confidence of the Lord. In Chapters Seven and Eight, I will give you some practical tips about how you can take action and not be subject to your feelings.

You Shall Receive Power

> but you will receive power when the Holy Spirit has come upon you; and you shall be My witnesses both in Jerusalem,

and in all Judea and Samaria, and even to the remotest part
of the earth.

Act 1:8

This passage predicts the coming of the Holy Spirit of God. He
comes to empower Christians to accomplish our calling – to make
disciples. Christ understood that the original group of disciples was weak
and frail men who were basically cowards. All but one of the disciples
deserted Him at the cross. Ever after He had appeared to them alive
from the dead, they were timid, fearful followers who were powerless to
accomplish the great command of making disciples of all the nations.
Only when the indwelling Holy Spirit came were they strong enough
to witnesses of Christ's resurrection and later to face torture and death.

Well of Water, Springing Up into Eternal Life

but whoever drinks of the water that I will give him shall
never thirst; but the water that I will give him will become in
him a well of water springing up to eternal life." This source
of power is compared to a well of water which springs up
within us even to eternal life.

John 4:14

This well cannot go dry in times of drought and is always near us since
it is actually a part of us.

The Holy Spirit is not a force as some cults teach. Some people
describe Him as a power or energy similar to "the force" in the movie,
Star Wars. Certainly, He does provide a supernatural power to all believers
so they will have the power and wisdom they need to accomplish God's
plans. But, the Holy Spirit is God; he is a personality with plans and
thoughts. Paul refers to Him as the Spirit of Christ in Romans 8:9.

Christ's Personal Presence with Us

> I will ask the Father, and He will give you another Helper,
> that He may be with you forever; that is the Spirit of truth,
> whom the world cannot receive, because it does not see
> Him or know Him, but you know Him because He abides
> with you and will be in you. I will not leave you as orphans;
> I will come to you.
>
> John 14:16–18

Jesus promised to come to the believers, and He did come on the day of Pentecost in Acts chapter two. He came in the form of the Holy Spirit as predicted in the verses above. The Holy Spirit is described in numerous places as a person; the Bible never describes Him as an inanimate object or force.

In the passage above from John 14, He is described as a Helper. Here are some more passages which prove the Holy Spirit is a person.

> Then Jesus was led up by the Spirit into the wilderness…
>
> Matthew 4:1a

> God is spirit…
>
> John 4:24a

> But the Helper, the Holy Spirit, whom the Father will send
> in My name, He will teach you all things, and bring to your
> remembrance all that I said to you.
>
> John 14:26

And He, when He comes, will convict the world concerning sin and righteousness and judgment...

John 16:8

But when He, the Spirit of truth, comes, He will guide you into all the truth; for He will not speak on His own initiative, but whatever He hears, He will speak; and He will disclose to you what is to come.

John 16:13

They passed through the Phrygian and Galatian region, having been forbidden by the Holy Spirit to speak the word in Asia...

Acts 16:6

Do not grieve the Holy Spirit of God, by whom you were sealed for the day of redemption.

Ephesians 4:30

These passages show that the Holy Spirit is a person because He has a will and thus takes action. These verses say He leads, guides, speaks, hears, discloses, forbids, helps, teaches, and reminds the believer. John 16:8 also states that He convicts unbelievers of sin, righteousness, and judgment. Finally, Ephesians 4:30, above, demonstrates that the Holy Spirit has feelings in that He can grieve. An inanimate object or mere force cannot take decisive action or experience emotions.

Power for Whatever We Face

Our faith is the primary ingredient needed to have victory over the world, our flesh, and the devil. We cannot overcome sin in our own strength.

God is able to do exceeding abundantly beyond all ask or think. This victory can and will be abundantly supplied to us as we exercise our faith. God has already made an infinite source of power available to us. This power emits from God Himself. This source of power is compared to a well of water which is springing up to within us and giving us a new and eternal life. This well cannot go dry in times of drought and is always near us since it is actually a part of us. In the previous chapters, we have talked a lot about the deception we are experiencing. In the next chapter, we will learn about the value of seeking out the truth and how to practically find it.

For a free video summary of this chapter by the author go online to www.dirtysecretsdirtylies.com and click on Free Videos.

6

Search Out the Truth

Truth Shall Make You Free

And you will know the truth, and the truth will make you free.
John 8:32

Amie and Jeremy had been married a few years, and they are expecting their fourth child. They are thrilled because it was going to be a little girl. They want to name her Jessica Rose after Amie's favorite flower and her mom. Amie was telling everyone "the good news," except her aunt Dana. Dana had been negative about Amie's growing family. She remembered the times Dana made negative comments about big families. Amie was dreading the next encounter with Dana. She played it out in her mind over and over. She would imagine going over to Dana's house and breaking the news to her. In her mind, Dana would blow up. Every time she thought about it, Amie became more stressed. One day, when Jeremy got home from work, Amie was sitting on the couch with a long face; she had been crying. Jeremy sat down beside her and gave her a big hug. He asked her what was wrong. Amie tearfully told him how she was dreading the next encounter with Dana. All at once Amie was angry, nervous, and timid about talking to Dana. She told Jeremy how she knew that Dana would really be hard on her about the new baby. She was also convinced that she could not tell her. She thought they should just let Dana find out on her own in due time. After a long time, she asked Jeremy what she should do. After patiently waiting to understand her feelings, Jeremy asked some questions. Instead of trying to convince her not to be upset, Jeremy took a different approach. He asked Amie what God thought about Jessica Rose. Of course, Amie gushed with enthusiasm and was convinced that the Lord was as thrilled about little Jessica Rose as they were. He then asked her whose opinion was more important, the Lord's or Dana's. Suddenly, Amie facial expression changed. She said, "You mean, I just need to be concerned about what the Lord thinks and not what others think?" "Right," Jeremy responded. Amie got so excited she threw her arms around him and said, "Now I remember why I love you so much. You are so wise!"

Amie's obstacle was that she did not trust that God would give her the strength, courage, wisdom and help to deal with conflict. A lack of trust can come from many sources. In Amie's case she had not gotten God's grace in her past dealings with Dana. She did not believe it would be any different this time. When faced with the potential conflict she did not seek the Lord's help. She routinely resorted to her old failing way of relating to Dana. God was waiting patiently all the time to reveal the truth about this situation, but Dana did not seek it out. Fortunately, her husband helped her understand the truth.

Jesus stated the concept very clearly, "...the truth shall make you free". Once we are familiar with our besetting sins, we learn and understand the truth about those sins in order to correct our lives. Sometimes it is really difficult to recognize if we have a besetting sin. Usually we are blind to our own weaknesses. In chapter eight, we will look at some practical information about how to evaluate our emotions and use them as indicators of our thought patterns. This exercise will be very helpful as we try to pinpoint the deceptions which are getting us into trouble.

Gird the Loins of Your Mind with Truth

> Stand firm therefore, HAVING GIRDED YOUR LOINS WITH TRUTH, and HAVING PUT ON THE BREASTPLATE OF RIGHTEOUSNESS,
>
> Ephesians 6:14

Obviously, in Bible times technology was not as advanced as it is today. Much of the work people did was very physical. Even though they had some simple machines, for the most part the heavy lifting was done by men and animals. In today's industrialized workplace specialized clothing such as hard hats and steel toed boots are standard work apparel. In those days as well their work clothing was designed to be functional.

At the time of Christ, Roman culture and traditions permeated much of life in southern Europe, northern Africa, and the Middle East. An example of this influence was the tunic. This Roman style of dress was the common work garment for men. Depending on the climate, the length of the tunic varied. Often the tunic was long, and it would hang down around the ankles. This longer, flowing garment would get in the way of the worker, slowing down his work. Perhaps it might trip him or snag on a nearby object.

Thus, whenever workers did active, strenuous labor, they pulled the long flowing tunic up around the waist and tied it. This exercise of girding became symbolic of doing seriousness work and of the determination of the worker. Thus, Christians are commanded to "gird up their loins with truth." Just as the belt gets the worker prepared for serious effort, God's truth pulls together the thoughts and beliefs of the Christian so he or she can firmly and confidently go about the work of the Lord. In another place in the Bible, Peter explains how our minds need to be fortified with truth so that we are not deceived by the lies of our adversary, the devil.

Prepare Your Mind for Action

> Therefore, prepare your minds for action, keep sober in spirit, fix your hope completely on the grace to be brought to you at the revelation of Jesus Christ."
>
> **1 Peter 1:13**

Here is a more literal way of translating this passage: "…gird the loins of your mind for action." This literal wording gives the word picture which Peter had in mind. Peter was a fisherman by trade, and he was well acquainted with the idea of girding his loins for work. In the familiar passage of John 21, Peter and his fellow disciple decided to go fishing. At dawn, after a long night of fishing, they saw a man on the shore. Of course, the man was our Lord Jesus Christ. Jesus urged them to cast the nets on the right side of the boat. They did and caught many fish. Notice what verse 7 says:

> Therefore that disciple whom Jesus loved said to Peter, 'It is the Lord.' So when Simon Peter heard that it was the Lord,

he put his outer garment on (for he was stripped for work),
and threw himself into the sea.

John 21:7

Peter was doing physical work, so he had taken off his formal clothes, and he was working with his loins girded.

In 1 Peter 1:23, Christians are urged to be ready to go to work for Christ. The preparation happens primarily in the mind. Like the long robes of the Romans which were an encumbrance to success, today Christians need to evaluate their actions and the beliefs behind those actions. We need to prepare our minds for action and remove any mental or emotional encumbrance. Like a good soldier, we need to be constantly prepared for action—every day and every hour. Let us move to another example.

Destin is a freshman in college. Since elementary school, he has had the habit of sleeping late. During the summer, he would stay up until 2 or 3 AM every night playing video games and sleep in until 11 or noon every morning. During the school year, he was constantly late for school and other commitments. For years he tried to get up on time and not be late, but never could muster the self-control needed to be consistent.

Now, he is in college, and he is having the same struggle. He has a 9 AM class on Monday, Wednesday, and Friday. For the first six weeks of the semester, he has been late or missed most of the class sessions. As a result, he has missed several quizzes, he is not learning the material, and his grades are suffering. Suddenly, he realized that unless something changed, he would fail the class. Fortunately, he had met Paul, the director of a campus ministry, and they became friends. During the first semester, God was really speaking to Destin's heart about following Christ. One day well into the semester, Paul asked Destin how school was going. Destin told him about the problem with sleeping late. Paul asked him if he had asked God to help him develop a habit of rising early to have time with God. Destin had never even considered that idea. It made great sense to him so that night Destin make a point of asking God to help him wake up to his alarm in the morning and starting the day right. When his alarm went off at 6 AM the next morning, Destin woke up like never before. He had a great time with God reading, praying and worshiping. He was on time for class and began the process of catching up on his work. When he went to bed that night, he once again asked God to help him wake up to the alarm and to be refreshed. This was the beginning of a habit that Destin continued to develop. Destin had been tricked into believing a lie—that he could never be consistent in getting up early. We also needed to be careful about what we are believing. Have we been listening to lies? And, we also need to practice the truths that God brings to us. The truth will make us free, but we need to meditate on it and put it into practice.

Speaking the Truth in Love

but speaking the truth in love, we are to grow up in all aspects into Him who is the head, even Christ."

Ephesians 4:15

Kobe had a bad habit of being sarcastic and using cutting remarks. At first, people would admire his wit. People liked him because Kobe had so much energy and was the life of every conversation. However, his friendships followed a sad pattern. He would make a new friend and things would go great, but quickly Kobe's sarcasm and hurtful remarks would alienate his new friend. However, Kobe had one long-term friend named Mick. Mick had stuck with Kobe through the years, but had recently even Mick was getting tired of Kobe's attitude and comments.

One day Mick realized that if he really cared about Kobe, he would have to confront Kobe. Mick knew his conversation with Kobe would not be pleasant, but he knew something had to be said. So, Mick decided to kindly tell Kobe the truth about why people were avoiding him. He prayed for Kobe and prepared for the discussion. The Lord gave Mick the right words to say. In the short-term, the conversation seemed like a failure, but in the long-run Kobe accepted what Mick had to say. Mick was successful because he put himself in Kobe's place and tried to see how he would feel. Even then, the discussion was very difficult for Kobe to accept. Kobe even made a few hurtful and sarcastic remarks during the conversation. Actually Kobe was very insulting. Fortunately, Mick had adequately prepared for the discussion, realizing that Kobe would probably not take it very well. All through the discussion, Mick stayed focused on seeking Kobe's best interest and forgiving him of the insults. Kobe abruptly ended the discussion and stormed off in anger. The next day Mick went over to Kobe's house. He found that Kobe had calmed down and realized that he had accepted most of what Mick had told him. Kobe even thanked Mick for telling him the truth—even though it was hard for Kobe to admit his mistakes. Kobe also asked Mick to forgive him for being so rude. Over time, they talked a great deal, and Kobe learned to use his tongue to build people up, rather than tear them down.

We are not always blessed to have someone like Mick in the example above. Usually we should expect to remind ourselves to be on the lookout for truth, in order to cement it into the very fabric of our being. Also we should seek to be like Mick who would speak the truth to others in the most loving way so it is accepted by them. Our challenge is to discover the truth relevant to our personal issues and then graft it into our thoughts and character. Finding the truth is the subject of the next segment.

What is Truth?

> Pilate said to Him, 'What is truth?'
>
> **John 18:38 a**

Have you ever heard the saying, "He wouldn't know the truth if it hit him in the face." Usually in this world of deception, it is really hard to discern the truth. Just today we received a forwarded email from a trusted friend stating that cell phone numbers were soon to be released to the public. I'm sure my friend thought she was doing us a favor notifying us about this. I went to the Federal Trade Commission website to see if this were really true. It wasn't true. It was one more scam to collect personal information about people. The email recommended a website where you could register to put name and phone number on a do not call list. What appeared to be true was merely an elaborate deception. Human nature hasn't changed since the times of Christ. Lies are masqueraded daily as truth with the naïve public bearing the brunt of the hoax.

Advertising can also be deceptive. TV commercials might not actually lie to us, but they can lead us to make false conclusions. A classic example is the auto ad which shows a young man driving a sports car and suddenly a beautiful young woman takes an extreme interest in him. The ad did not a promise of a beautiful girlfriend, if you buy the car, but the possibility was certainly implied. Politicians and business executives sometimes exercise "spin control".

In the next section we see how Christ valued truthfulness and integrity.

Nathanael – No Deceit

> Jesus saw Nathanael coming to Him, and said of him, 'Behold, an Israelite indeed, in whom there is no deceit.'"
>
> **John 1:47b**

Can you imagine receiving such a marvelous compliment from Christ? Nathanael was declared to be truthful and honest by Jesus—who embodied truth.

Flattery, a Selfish Form or Deception

> The Apostle Jude warns about those who "...speak arrogantly, flattering people for the sake of gaining an advantage."
>
> **Jude 1:16b**

Flattery is another form of deception. It involves insincere compliments. Flattery is seeking to gain favor with someone in order to take unfair advantage of them. In Proverbs chapter 7, Solomon warns us to be careful of the adulterous woman. She is insincere and deceptive. Her strategy of deception is largely embodied in flattery of the unsuspecting man. Solomon goes on to say that the man who believes her flattery will ultimately be destroyed. He will lose all that he values.

In contrast, Nathanael was not a flatterer. Instead, his painstaking honesty gained Christ's respect. Have you ever flattered someone in order to gain an advantage? It's easy to do, but eventually the truth will come out and distrust will come in.

Jesus is the Truth

> Jesus said to him, 'I am the way, and the truth, and the life;
> no one comes to the Father but through Me.
>
> **John 14:6**

In contrast to the flatterer, Jesus is the embodiment of truth. Not only did He speak truthfully, His entire life was the truth. His motives were always pure. His words and intensions were never designed to trick or defraud anyone. The Bible says that He is the perfect reflection of the true and accurate nature of the heavenly Father. (See Colossians 1:15)

In Scripture, truth and light are often considered to be the same. Light reveals things which are hidden. Often in the Bible, things which are dark or hidden are dangerous, hurtful, or destructive. I remember one night years ago, I got up in the middle of the night. I had the room memorized, so I never even considered turning the light. While taking my regular path, I found someone had placed a trunk in our room. My small pinky toe connected with it. Man did that hurt! I hobbled back to bed in great agony. When I awoke the next morning my toe was still aching. When I got up to walk on it, I couldn't put any weight on it. Finally, my wife convinced me that I should go to the doctor. I did and found that I had broken my toe. (I **really** kicked the trunk hard!) He wrapped up the toes and put me in a special open-ended shoe and made me walk with crutches. I had to be on crutches for a few weeks.

Just like I needed a light that night, we need the truth. It is a light helping us find the right path. Without truth shining into our lives, we will miss the dangers which are looming out there to do us harm. Truth comes to us in many ways.

Truth and trust are usually intertwined. If we believe we have discovered truth, we often act upon what we believe is true. It is usually easiest to believe what we hear if it seems reasonable. Usually, we should have a touch of skepticism about the things we hear. We can save ourselves a lot of grief, if we force ourselves to do our research before we believe and act on an assumption. I am always surprised about how gullible I am, how quickly I believe that I want to believe, and not seek out an objective viewpoint to make sure I am not being tricked. In Chapter 11, we will look at practical insights into how to discover truth and evaluate circumstances to uncover the deceptions.

In this chapter, we have discussed our need to search out the truth and embrace it. Believing a lie is always harmful. In the next chapter, we will learn how to integrate the truth into our will through godly affirmations.

For a free video summary of this chapter by the author go online to www.dirtysecretsdirtylies.com and click on Free Videos.

7

Act on What You Know is True

An Attribute of God – He Makes Choices

In the beginning God created the heavens and the earth.

Genesis 1:1

From the very beginning of the Bible, we find God exercising His will. The problem is that God's will has been questioned by humans and by Satan from the beginning of time. For example, Satan created confusion in Eve's mind about God's will in Gen 3:1c: "Indeed, has God said, 'You shall not eat from any tree of the garden'?" From a simple reading of the Bible it is obvious that God has a will – He makes plans, and He has specific plans for our lives. In the New Testament alone the phrase "the will of God" is mentioned 23 times!

The details of God's will have been debated by people, but that is not our concern at this moment.

Fortunately, the subject of this chapter is not to determine in all cases what the will of God is, but to humbly accept that God has plans and intensions for us as individuals and for the human race as a whole. Though we often do not understand the details of God's plans, it is clear in the Bible that God knows what His doing. In the Bible, much of God's will has already been revealed to us.

The Greek language of the New Testament has a few words which we translate "word." Two of them are most important. The first Greek work is λόγος, logos. It means a general teaching, a communication, a saying and a truth. It has been used to describe a teaching, a discourse, and any written or spoken communication to individuals or to the public. In John 1:1, Jesus is described as the Word of God, meaning He was the precise communication of God; not only in what He said, but through everything He did. The Bible is also called the Word of God. In the Bible, we have a very clear communication to us about a vast number of subjects. We are told how to treat other people and how we should respect, love and honor Him. We can learn a great deal about God and His will by carefully and thoughtfully reading the Bible.

The other Greek word translated "word" in English is ῥῆμα, rhema. When rhema is used it means a direct communication from God to an individual. Here is a Biblical example:

in the high priesthood of Annas and Caiaphas, the word of God came to John, the son of Zacharias, in the wilderness. And he came into all the district around the Jordan, preaching a baptism of repentance for the forgiveness of sins;

Luke 3:2–3

In this passage John the Baptist got a direct message from God to go into the district around the Jordan River to preach the baptism of repentance for the forgiveness of sins. God did not give this rhema (word) to anyone else. It was a specific command to John the Baptist.

Some people think that God only spoke directly to individuals during Bible times. I disagree with this conclusion. Please review the following passage:

> And take THE HELMET OF SALVATION, and the sword of the Spirit, which is the word of God.
>
> **Ephesians 6:17**

Rhema in this passage is the same Greek work used when God spoke to John the Baptist. God wants us to regularly seek to hear his voice in our hearts. He wants to speak to us and give us a personal rhema for our lives and circumstances. According to Ephesians 6:17 above, we need to hear God's specific message to us, as we go out into spiritual battle. It is our sword of the Spirit.

God's Will is Perfect

> And do not be conformed to this world, but be transformed by the renewing of your mind, so that you may prove what the will of God is, that which is good and acceptable and perfect.
>
> **Romans 12:2**

Searching for the perfect will of God is an adventure in itself. God loves to reveal Himself to His people, but He wants us to seek Him. Several passages come to mind.

It is the glory of God to conceal a matter, but the glory of
kings is to search out a matter.

Proverbs 25:2

God's will is not always obvious to us. God delights in revealing
Himself to people as they seek Him. As we understand the will of God
it is our challenge to integrate it into the very fabric of our lives. Jesus
said in Matthew 26:42d, "Not my will but thine be done." Jesus sought
His Father's will, the Father revealed the perfect plan of redemption of
mankind and the eternal glorification of Christ at the right hand of
the Father.

Here's the story of Brittany, a college sophomore, who is trying to
understand God's will for her life. While attending a chapel service,
she noticed Jason, a very charismatic young man. After meeting
him that day, she was sure that Jason was the one for her. For years,
Brittany has been seeking God's will for her life and trying to avoid
quick responses to situations. So, in this situation, she asked God to
guide her. She had peace from God that she should observe how Jason
handled his relationships with the other women students. She felt that
God was telling her to see how Jason treated other women. She carefully
watched him go from one relationship to another. In every case, he left
a heartbroken woman behind. After about six months, the Lord made
it clear to her that Jason was not the one for her, and she was spared
deep heartache. It took a little time, but as Brittany sought the Lord, He
made His will know to her.

God's Will is Made Known

He made known to us the mystery of His will, according to
His kind intention which He purposed in Him.

Ephesians 1:9

In the passage above, we see that God revealed His will, but in the past, it was a mystery. God made His plans long ago, but only recently has He revealed it. There are many examples in the Bible of God stating that He will do something and then brings it to pass. In the next sections, we will look at examples of this. These examples also have practical application; we need to carefully move from making good choices, expressing our plans, and then moving forward and acting on those plans.

God States His Will

In the Bible, there are hundreds of examples of God stating that He will do something and then the narrative shows that He did it. This begins in the earliest chapters of Genesis; God decides to do something, He states it, and then He does it. Here are some early Biblical examples.

> Then the LORD God said, "It is not good for the man to be alone; **I will** make him a helper suitable for him."
>
> Genesis 2:18

> And **I will** put enmity between you and the woman, and between your seed and her seed; He shall bruise you on the head, and you shall bruise him on the heel."
>
> Genesis 3:15

> To the woman He said, "**I will** greatly multiply your pain in childbirth, in pain you will bring forth children; yet your desire will be for your husband, and he will rule over you."
>
> Genesis 3:16

I have put the "I will" in bold text above so it is easy for you to notice it. In every case, God made a conscious choice, stated His will, and carried it out. From these passages and hundreds others like it we can see that it is God's normal practice to do this. (If you would like to see how many times and where these verses can be found, do a word search in a Bible software, keying in the words "I will." The results will come up. I personally use a web based program for these types of searches. The website is www.blueletterbible.org.) The reason we have a will is because God made us in His image.

In the Image of God

> God created man in His own image, in the image of God He created him; male and female He created them.
>
> **Genesis 1:27**

We need to carefully study well-known passages like this one. Here we are reminded that mankind is created in the image of God. Even though sin has entered the world, mankind is still created in the image of God. We are tainted, but we are made in the image of God. One of those characteristics is our free will. We, like God, have the ability to choose our direction in life. We have many desires and longings which often get us into trouble, but a desire can be a good thing. When we become Christians, our minds and desires are transformed. We gain the supernatural power to fulfill godly wishes and not be slaves to selfish desires (as I have already discussed in chapter 5).

Another characteristic of God which all of us humans manifest is that God talks to Himself. You may find this fascinating and even a little unbelievable. I certainly did when I first understood it. I never realized it fully until I researched the subject in the Bible. There are many examples of God talking to Himself. Here is just one below.

> Because he has loved Me, therefore **I will** deliver him; **I will** set him securely on high, because he has known My name.

He will call upon Me, and **I will** answer him; **I will** be with him in trouble; **I will** rescue him and honor him. With a long life **I will** satisfy him And let him see My salvation.

Psalms 91:14–16

In this Psalm alone God speaks to Himself in the affirmative stating He will do something. (I have put "I will" in bold text for emphasis.) In every case God made a choice and told Himself what He would do.

In this same Psalm, David practices the same thing God does with his "I Wills". (See Below)

I will say to the LORD, "My refuge and my fortress, My God, in whom I trust."

Psalms 91:2

There are also many cases in the Bible where a godly writer, speaking with determination says, "I will." Here are a few examples.

Teach me Your way, O LORD; **I will** walk in Your truth; Unite my heart to fear Your name.

Psalms 86:11

I will give thanks to You, O Lord my God, with all my heart, And **will glorify** Your name forever.

Psalms 86:12

A Maskil of Ethan the Ezrahite. **I will** sing of the lovingkindness of the LORD forever; To all generations **I will** make known Your faithfulness with my mouth.

Psalm 89:1

A Psalm of David. **I will** sing of lovingkindness and justice, To You, O LORD, **I will** sing praises.

Psalms 101:1

I will give heed to the blameless way. When will You come to me? **I will** walk within my house in the integrity of my heart.

Psalms 101:2

I will set no worthless thing before my eyes; I hate the work of those who fall away; It shall not fasten its grip on me.

Psalms 101:3

Here are six passages where the writer emphatically states he will do something godly. There are hundreds of other examples of this practice in the Bible.

What did these godly writers know that we 21st century Christians have either forgotten or never knew? They knew the power of committing themselves VERBALLY to doing the will of God. These affirmations cement our commitments to the Lord and change our negative emotions to positive ones. Somehow as our brains hear what our mouth is saying, our emotions change and fall into line with the emotions (fruit) of the Spirit. (love, joy, peace, patience, kindness, compassion, thankfulness... the list goes on and on.)

When I was growing up, our church sang the song, "I have decided to follow Jesus." We also sang, "I am resolved no longer to linger, charmed by the worlds delights." Another one was, "I know whom I have believed, and am persuaded that He is able to keep what I've committed to Him against that day."

These powerful Christian affirmations of yesteryear have all but vanished from the current praise music of today. Not to say anything bad about praise music, sadly it was greatly neglected in the early 20th century. Now the pendulum has swayed the other way and the great hymns of resolution and affirmation have not been replaced with their 21st century counterparts.

In the Scriptures we can find both praise and affirmations in abundance. Both are required to have a healthy spiritual life. I have asked many people if they practice the verbal commitments of their faith to God in a daily way. Very few are practicing these affirmations. Their failure to overcome their besetting sins is directly tied to this neglected discipline.

Some have told me that they are unwilling to verbally speak their "I wills" to God, because they are afraid of failing to keep their promises. I certainly can understand that concern, but fear and timidity are never good excuses to shy away from speaking our commitments to God. The psalmists were confident and bold. Other than our Lord Jesus, the apostle Paul is the New Testament character we know the most about. His voluminous New Testament writing and the book of Acts paint the picture of Paul the confident Apostle who lived in a human shell just like us. Constantly we are reminded of the outstandingly heroic things he did but also the failing emotional state he constantly battled. No wonder, Paul is the most prolific affirmer in the New Testament. He said things like...

I can do all things through Him who strengthens me.
Philippians 4:13

And my God will supply all your needs according to His riches in glory in Christ Jesus.
Philippians 4:19

For this reason I also suffer these things, but I am not ashamed; for I know whom I have believed and I am convinced that He is able to guard what I have entrusted to Him until that day.

2 Timothy 1:12

in the future there is laid up for me the crown of righteousness, which the Lord, the righteous Judge, will award to me on that day; and not only to me, but also to all who have loved His appearing.

2 Timothy 4–8

The Lord will rescue me from every evil deed, and will bring me safely to His heavenly kingdom; to Him be the glory forever and ever. Amen.

2 Timothy 4:18

We need to verbally express our faith in and our commitment to God. This is one of the most powerful weapons you have in your spiritual arsenal. With the words of faith, three times Jesus defeated the attacks of Satan in Matthew chapter four.

Christians Should State What They Are Not Going to Do
Here are a few passages where the psalmist declares he will not participate in something evil. Declaring what you will not do is just as important as declaring what you will do.

I will not be afraid of ten thousands of people who have set themselves against me round about.

Psalms 3:6

He says to himself, "I will not be moved; Throughout all generations I will not be in adversity."

Psalms 10:6

I have set the LORD continually before me; Because He is at my right hand, I will not be shaken.

Psalms 16:8

I hate the assembly of evildoers, and I will not sit with the wicked.

Psalms 26:5

Lest you think this is just an Old Testament teaching, we are instructed in Titus to "...deny ungodliness and worldly desire..."

Titus 2:12a

Discussion of Will Power

Choosing to speak our commitment to either do God's will or to resist the world, flesh or the devil is an essential part of having lasting victory over sin. I have never met a believer who consistently overcame sin who did not practice this discipline in some form. However, I am always reluctant to use the word discipline in any discussion of overcoming sin, because the first reaction of some people is that I am promoting a type of legalism. Just for the record, discipline is also described in other places as self-control. Of course even the most elementary Bible study will reveal that self-control is a fruit of the Spirit. It is something God produces in the Christian as he submits his will to God. As God's controls our lives, we exhibit self-control over all of our ungodly passions.

Another important passage relating to self-control and discipline is 1 Timothy 4:7–16.

> But have nothing to do with worldly fables fit only for old women. On the other hand, discipline yourself for the purpose of godliness; for bodily discipline is only of little profit, but godliness is profitable for all things, since it holds promise for the present life and also for the life to come. It is a trustworthy statement deserving full acceptance. For it is for this we labor and strive, because we have fixed our hope on the living God, who is the Savior of all men, especially of believers. Prescribe and teach these things. Let no one look down on your youthfulness, but rather in speech, conduct, love, faith and purity, show yourself an example of those who believe. Until I come, give attention to the public reading of Scripture, to exhortation and teaching. Do not neglect the spiritual gift within you, which was bestowed on you through prophetic utterance with the laying on of hands by the presbytery. Take pains with these things; be absorbed in them, so that your progress will be evident to all. Pay close attention to yourself and to your teaching; persevere in these things, for as you do this you will ensure salvation both for yourself and for those who hear you.
>
> **1 Timothy 4:7–16**

This powerful passage deals with attitudes, actions, methods and goal setting. In a practical way it shapes the behavior of the believer as he wholeheartedly seeks to become godly. Godliness is an allusive thing. Godliness is not merely the outward behavior of godly character; it is also a pure and unadulterated devotion to God. Loving

Him supremely and loving others as ourselves undergird the very foundations of godliness. Firmly behind the veneer of actions must be a heart of devotion to the Savior. The manifestation of every thought and action is to be examined in the light of our true motivation to please Him or to please others or ourselves.

Paul, the writer, in 1 Timothy 4:7–16 above compares the spiritual development with physical development. He exhorts Timothy to discipline himself for the purpose of godliness. The word discipline here in the Greek is γυμνάζω, or transliterated *gymnazō* from which we get the English idea, to train in a gym. In this verse, Paul is instructing Timothy to execute a spiritual training program so he can get into shape spiritually.

When we are new to athletics, we need a coach who will come along side us and help us devise an exercise and strength training program to prepare us to compete in the athletic games. As the athlete progresses in life he understands what needs to be done in the training program and needs less help with the fundamentals. The coach can work with him more on the strategy of the game and the technical execution of the strategies. As time goes along, the coach helps with the mental aspect of the game including strategy, motivation and inspiration.

The mark of a mature believer in Christ is that he has the ability to set up and execute his own training program to become godly. He understands the issues he is facing and the weaknesses and limitations which must be overcome. He also understands and is inspired to accomplish the goal and purpose which the Lord has personally spoken into his life. He is now in control of the learning and training process which will propel him to become successful as a believer.

In the passage above Paul says it is "for it is for this we labor and strive…" At this point, Paul points out that becoming godly is what we should all be laboring and striving for. Labor and strive are translated from interesting and insightful Greek words.

Labor: κοπιάω, or kopiao means to labor to the point of exhaustion. In Luke 5:5, it was used to describe the disciples who were fishermen toiling all night to make a catch of fish.

Strive: ἀγωνίζομαι, or transliterated into English agōnizomai, from which we get the English word agony. It means to strive in an athletic contest or warfare. The word was in John 18:36 when Christ was speaking to Pilate. Jesus said, "…My kingdom is not of this world: if my kingdom were of this world, then would my servants fight (agōnizomai), that I should not be delivered to the Jews: but now is my kingdom not from hence."

So from this verse and the definitions mentioned above, we can see that becoming godly is not going to be easy. It is actually going to be a struggle which takes great effort and work. It will be exhausting, and it will be a struggle which will cause us much agony. Even though the struggle will be hard, the benefits will be even greater as mentioned above, "…but godliness is profitable for all things, since it holds promise for the present life and also for the life to come."

In verse 11 above, Paul instructs Timothy to, "Prescribe and teach these things." This goal of equipping others to train themselves in godliness is the normal product of the mature Christian. It should be a major focus of our ministry.

Additionally, Paul calls on Timothy to take godliness to the next level. In verse 12, he requires not only godliness, but exemplary godliness in speech, conduct, love, faith and purity. Think of it this way. God wants us to be so godly that the people around us notice it and comment on it. What if you were so godly that your wife noticed it? Maybe she would say, "You are the most loving person I know. I'm so proud of you." Or what if your kids said, "Dad is the most outstanding example of faith I have ever seen. He is such an inspiration to me."? This is Paul's point.

In the closing passage of the text, he reminds Timothy that this transformation happens through discipline, "…give attention to the public reading of Scripture, to exhortation and teaching. Do not neglect the spiritual gift within you ..."

Progress Happens with Action and Accountability

Additionally he urges him to, "...take pains with these things; be absorbed in them, so that your progress will be evident to all." There is tremendous benefit to the people around you to see your progress. It is inspirational and instructional. Never underestimate the old adage, "More is caught then taught."

Preparation for the Day

Much of this chapter is an encouragement to set in motion a mental and spiritual discipline which is necessary to produce godly character. We need preparation. Every commanding general knows that the night before the battle is usually the difference between victory and defeat. The wise general takes the intelligence gathered from his troops, his scouts, his spies, his understanding of the day's skirmish, his appraisal of his own army's strengths and weaknesses as well as this adversary's condition. From there he formulates a plan for the coming day's battle. Early in the morning of battle, he gives his final orders and plans for his army to execute.

How often do we merely take a casual interest in the coming day's spiritual struggle? How often do we become a victim of our spiritual adversary's attack instead of being the one who is wreaking havoc of Satan's plans? Isn't it time we stood up for our Savior's cause and fought the good fight of faith, claiming spiritual territory for His kingdom? Isn't it time we become examples of godliness which all can see and be inspired by? I think so. Won't you take this matter seriously and begin to affirm daily to God, yourself and the world that you will pursue righteousness, godliness and faith with those who call upon on Lord with a pure heart? Won't you daily affirm that you will set no ungodly thing before your eyes and will not be influenced by the world, the flesh an the devil to sin? This new found purpose will take great discipline with a system of personal accountability for the desire result. (See chapter ten for a discussion on personal accountability.) I trust you will rise to the occasion and become an example of the believer in godliness.

There are numerous examples of how faith, actions and emotions are intertwined. In Chapter eight, we will look at some practical tips about how to solidify our faith and emotions with action. We will look at the correlation of emotions to thoughts and actions. In addition, we will learn how to enjoy the positive emotions of life even in the midst of difficult circumstances.

or a free video summary of this chapter by the author go online to www.dirtysecretsdirtylies.com and click on Free Videos.

8

Solidify Your Faith and Emotions with Action

Alex has been a Christian long enough that the "new" has worn off. But, he is struggling with the basics. Lately, he has been wondering: "Why does life always have to be so hard?" He is struggling with an old habit—stealing. He had been in prison for it, and that was where he trusted Christ. While in prison, a minister from a local church shared the Gospel with him, and he trusted Christ. For a year now, he has been out of prison and living up to his terms of probation. He even has a job, though it had been hard to get work with a felony conviction. It wasn't a very good paying job, but at least it was an honest living. It was a far cry from what he had before, when he was dealing drugs and picking up things which didn't belong to him. Anyway, the law caught up with him. He did his time, and now he was out, but it was still a struggle. He kept thinking about how easy money came when he was dealing drugs and stealing when he needed some cash. The more he thought about it, the more he wanted to fix his financial problems fast.

What advice should we give him? He feels a strong urge to go back into a life of crime?

Same Old Story

As we have already discussed in chapter four, emotions out-of-control have been a part of the human experience almost from the beginning. For sake of reference I will re-quote Genesis 4:1–8. It is the account of the struggle Cain had with his emotions.

> Now the man had relations with his wife Eve, and she conceived and gave birth to Cain, and she said, "I have gotten a manchild with the help of the LORD." Again, she gave birth to his brother Abel. And Abel was a keeper of flocks, but Cain was a tiller of the ground. So it came about in the course of time that Cain brought an offering to the LORD of the fruit of the ground. Abel, on his part also brought of the firstlings of his flock and of their fat portions. And the LORD had regard for Abel and for his offering; but for Cain and for his offering He had no regard. So Cain became very angry and his countenance fell. Then the LORD said to Cain, "Why are you angry? And why has your countenance fallen? "If you do well, will not your countenance be lifted up? And if you do not do well, sin is crouching at the door; and its desire is for you, but you must master it." Cain told Abel his brother. And it came about when they were in the field, that Cain rose up against Abel his brother and killed him.
>
> **Genesis 4:1–8**

In chapter four I addressed how you can use negative emotions to identify the problem you are facing. In this chapter I want to expand on that idea and give you some practical instructions about how to use your faith and positive actions to change your negative emotions into powerful positive ones. Through your faith and actions you can overcome the passion which enslaves you!

You all have read or heard this story. This is the story of man who allowed his emotions to get the better of him. Cain became angry over a relatively minor issue and it caused him grave consequences. Passions have been controlling mankind for thousands of years. Similar accounts of malice are played out daily all over the world with the same results.

God understood the power of passion and tried to head off the dire consequences. He knew what would happen if allowed to go unchecked. When Cain's offering was rejected by God, Cain became angry. The Bible says his countenance fell. In other words, he pouted, frowned and became depressed. It is true that some depression is caused by physiological issues, but most depression results from anger which is unresolved. Cain's reaction was based on his pride. He wanted everyone (including God) to submit to his plans. Cain was not willing to accept that God's right and authority to set the rules about sacrifices. Cain wanted to play by his own rules. He did not want to view himself as the creature and view God as the boss. If Cain had been humble, he could have asked God for forgiveness and for wisdom about what to do. He could have easily done that. God opened the door to rebuilding the relationship when He asked, "Why are you angry." God knew why he was angry. The question was asked for Cain's good, to help him understand that his viewpoint was skewed. If he had asked God for a solution, it would have been very easy for God to suggest that he trade some of his vegetables for one of Abel's lambs. Thus he would have an acceptable sacrifice. Instead, Cain, full of pride, chose his own way. He allowed his pride to control him and his passion to make him feel justified in rebelling. God gave him every opportunity to conquer his pride. He told him, "If you do well, will not your countenance be lifted up? And if you do not do well, sin is crouching at the door; and its desire is for you, but you must master it."

Do the Right Thing

This is the daily dilemma we face. Have you ever said or thought to yourself,

I'm so mad, I could kill him.

I'll show her. How do you spell REVENGE?

I'm in love with him. I know he's married, but it feels so right.

I'm going to take this from the office, they owe it to me. They don't value all I do for them.

My buddy, Steve, is dealing drugs. Look at all he has—fast cars, good-looking women and a wad of cash. If he can do it, so can I.

Very often when we go wrong, strong emotions play a major part. No wonder God told Cain, "If you do well, will not your countenance be lifted up? And if you do not do well, sin is crouching at the door; and its desire is for you, but you must master it." We need to realize that wrong thinking leads to negative, powerful emotions which left unchecked always leads to wrong and destructive words and actions?

Jesus, for the Joy Set Before Him

Therefore, since we have so great a cloud of witnesses surrounding us, let us also lay aside every encumbrance and the sin which so easily entangles us, and let us run with endurance the race that is set before us, fixing our eyes on Jesus, the author and perfecter of faith, who for the joy set

before Him endured the cross, despising the shame, and
has sat down at the right hand of the throne of God.

Hebrews 12:1–2

An example of extreme emotions is seen when Jesus Christ prayed in
the Garden of Gethsemane. We cannot imagine the extreme stress Jesus
was experiencing in the hours leading up to the crucifixion. In all of His
humanness, He did not want to experience the extreme agony of the
torture, humiliation, exhaustion and death connected to a criminal's
execution. Of course, it isn't possible to completely get into His mind
since He is God incarnate, but we understand that this was to be the
darkest day in all of eternal history. This day was the day that all the
sin and rebellion of all mankind and of all the ages was to be placed
on Him. He would become the very most repulsive thing which the
Godhead loathed. Luke 22:44a says that He was in agony.

"...His sweat became like drops of blood, falling down
upon the ground."

Luke 22:44c.

This was by far the most stressful, emotionally charged moment
in all of history. How did Jesus endure this extreme emotional state?
Hebrews 12:2, quoted above, states that He had an inner joy, which
transcended the agony. This joy was formed through Christ's conscious
and deliberate choice of focusing on the joy that would come later as He
visualized his endurance and triumph over death and the grave.

Obviously from Jesus' example above, a person's negative emotions
are not always caused by his or her sins. In this section we see that Jesus
experienced the strong negative emotion of distress in His circumstances
without allowing it to control Him. He went beyond His present
circumstances to take hold of the supernatural power He needed to face

the most frightening and distressing part of His life. He considered the fact that He would bring many people to glory with Him. Christ is truly the author of faith and the one who lived out His life in perfect harmony with His faith. Certainly He is our model and inspiration.

My Joy May be in You and Your Joy Complete

> Until now you have asked for nothing in My name; ask and you will receive, so that your joy may be made full.
> John 16:24

That fateful night in the Garden of Gethsemane over 2000 years ago was preceded by a very special time with the disciples in the upper room a few hours before. At that time, Jesus knew that His time was limited with the group. He knew that He was facing imminent torture and death, but He had the presence of mind to instruct His followers about the very same type of emotional issues He was about to experience. In the passage above Jesus is urging the disciples (and us too) to exercise faith. Knowing that God has an ultimate plan, we can experience a joy and peace from God.

There is a clear connection between the action of faith which leads to hope and joy. Without faith and godly action hope cannot be experienced and joy will not come.

Shame, Guilt, Anger, Anxiety, and Depression

Marshal was an elderly grandfather of seven adorable grandchildren. He got to see his grandchildren often. They were the joy of his life. Sadly though most encounters with them were very strained, because ... you see, Marshal had not been a good father. Whenever he saw the grandkids, he also saw his children. Every time he saw his kids he was painfully reminded of how he had hurt them. Marshal was being eaten alive by the guilt and shame whenever he meet with his children. There was a distance in his relationships with his children because of the pain he had caused years ago. His children felt the distance also. They avoided contact with him, but when they did speak there was often harshness in their words. Sometimes, they attacked him for his mistakes in the past. As time went on Marshal's anger over the rejection swelled into full-blown resentment. He found himself constantly accusing himself of being the "worst dad in the world" or defending himself saying, "Yes, I did not treat them right, but they don't understand what I was going through. I wasn't nearly as bad as I could have been." The constant torments over his failure as a father bred anxiety and eventually panic attacks. It seemed every time he thought about seeing the grandkids, his heart would race with fear of yet another confrontation with his children. As he experienced these times of anxiety more frequently, he lost all hope that these issues would ever be resolved. Worst of all, he feared being rejected by the grandchildren as well. The constant fear of losing the grandchildren sent him headlong into depression. At the depths of his depression, he sought to take action which would end the misery. He considered physical violence against his children, especially the two which caused him so much grief, but he knew he would lose the grandkids for sure then. He felt the kids deserved to die for all the pain they had brought him. He knew that was not a real solution to his raw emotions. Finally, he concluded, the only action he had left was to end his misery and take his own life. What a tragic ending to the life of a man who allowed his emotions to control him instead of faith. God could have changed the outcome, had he exercised his faith.

King Ahab and the Vegetable Garden
The Old Testament stories about King Ahab and Queen Jezebel are fascinating. These stories deserve in-depth study. They give great insights

into human nature and the way a country goes when its leaders turn away from the Lord.

First, we need to understand the selfishness of King Ahab. The full story of his selfishness is found in 1 Kings 21:1–16. Here are just a few of the high points. Ahab wanted the convenience of a vegetable garden next to the palace in Jezrell. There was a vineyard next to the palace which he thought would make a good place for the garden. Only problem was that it was owned by his neighbor, Naboth. Ahab offered him a price for the vineyard, but Naboth refused, stating that the Lord had forbidden him to sell his inheritance. Naboth's rejection of his offer made Ahab mad. His anger turned to sullenness, and he retreated to his room to pout.

His wife, Jezebel came into the room and immediately asked him why he was sullen. (Sullen is another word for depressed.) Ahab explained that Naboth had rejected his offer. Jezebel immediately decided to get the vineyard for Ahab. She wrote letters in Ahab's name declaring a fast and set Naboth at the head of the people. Before the meeting she arranged for two worthless liars to come in and falsely testify against Naboth stating, "Naboth cursed God and the king". After hearing the testimony the crowd took Naboth out and stoned him to death. When Jezebel heard that Naboth was dead, she told Ahab. She encouraged him to take possession of the vineyard and so he did.

Ahab never intended to kill Naboth. He didn't realize that his unresolved anger would result in depression and ultimately murder. All of this awful destruction was caused by a foolish desire for a vegetable garden.

Anger, Wrath, Malice, Slander and Abusive Speech

But now you also, put them all aside: anger, wrath, malice, slander, and abusive speech from your mouth.

Colossians 3:8

It's not surprising that the sequence mentioned in the account of Ahab and Naboth is typical of human experience. It is played out repeatedly through history. Everything we need to understand about the human condition is found neatly wrapped in the Bible, which anyone can easily read in a year without too much strain.

Here is the sequence of unchecked negative emotions in case you missed it:

In the Old Testament account above Naboth rejected Ahab's offer. This rejection led to anger. In the same way we usually get angry when we or our desires are rejected in some way. Anger leads to wrath, wrath leads to depression, and depression leads to malice, either directed toward ourselves or others, or sometimes both.

Negative Emotions are Symptoms of a Root Problem

Before we leave this subject, we need to realize that there is a pattern here.

First, we have an underlying wrong attitude; it leads to a wrong action, which leads to a negative emotion, which leads to a destructive behavior.

To understand our root problems we must start by viewing our emotions more objectively. This is hard, but when we determine our feelings, we can trace them back to the attitude or action which is causing the emotion. Sometimes it is almost impossible to think objectively in the midst of the situation when we are controlled by our negative emotions. It's always helpful to ask a trusted friend, counselor or spouse to help us trace back the root from the negative emotions we are exhibiting. To help us identify our feelings here is a partial list of negative emotions.

Abandoned	Dread	Loss
Afraid	Embarrassed	Manipulated
Alone	Empty	Melancholy
Angry	Envy	Neglected
Annoyed	Exhausted	Pressure
Anxious	Fearful	Rage
Arrogance	Frightened	Rejected
Ashamed	Frustrated	Resentment
Betrayed	Grief	Sad
Boredom	Guilty	Scared
Cheated	Heartbroken	Self-pity
Confused	Helpless	Shame
Defeated	Hopeless	Threatened
Depression	Humiliated	Tired
Deprived	Hurt	Trapped
Despair	Ignoble	Troubled
Disappointed	Impatient	Uncertain
Discouraged	Inadequate	Uncontrolled Desire
Disgusted	Infuriated	Unappreciated
Dissatisfaction	Irritated	Unloved
Distress	Jealous	Unmotivated
Drained	Lonely	Unsure

More Blessed to Give than to Receive

In everything I showed you that by working hard in this manner you must help the weak and remember the words of the Lord Jesus, that He Himself said, 'It is more blessed to give than to receive.'

Acts 20:35

Joy can be found in odd places. Here is an unexpected place to find Joy that you may have never considered. Giving, which we normally think of as a drain, is really a source of energy. Sometimes in our lives there just isn't enough money at the end of the month to go around. That has certainly been the case at times for our family. One Christmas we really could not afford buying gifts for our growing family of five children and two adults. With one income, things were really tight. I remember asking my wife, Brenda, what she wanted for Christmas, and she said, "I just want some money." I thought, that's cool, now I don't have to go shopping. I told her how much money I could give and put it into her Christmas stocking. Later, when Christmas came, I was surprised by the number of presents we had for the kids. To my surprise, Brenda had been squirreling away money she had received for her birthday and other occasions, so she could buy gifts for the children. She even bought gifts knowing that I would give her some cash in her stocking. When I asked her about it later, she simply said, "…it is more blessed to give than to receive. My joy and happiness is giving to the ones I love." Her commitment to giving and to loving has always been an inspiration to me. This section is dedicated to her. Many of us have heard this saying, but few have experienced it the way she has. Our emotions respond positively to the good things we do.

In Chapter Nine, you will learn how to substitute the negative for the positive and how the transformation takes place.

For a free video summary of this chapter by the author go online to www.dirtysecretsdirtylies.com and click on Free Videos.

9

Substitute the Positive for the Negative

Jesus: The Game Changer

Have you heard it said?
"Just live by the Ten Commandments and everything will be OK."

What's wrong with that statement? The problem is that for millennia people have been trying to do that and have been failing. I've heard people say that insanity is trying the same thing over and over again, expecting different results.

Jesus really was the game changer. He set in motion a whole new way of living. The conventional wisdom of His day was to regulate righteousness by the letter so that everything was defined as right or wrong. In the next section I will explain how God's Ten Commandments were expanded into a detailed moral and civil code.

Moses the Regulator

Do you remember the Bible stories about the plagues in Egypt and about Moses leading the Jewish people through the Red Sea? After those events, God spoke to Moses on Mount Sinai. God gave the people the Ten Commandments and many other rules for starting a new nation. There were rules about sanitation, about inheritance, settling disputes, and many other topics. Starting in Exodus 20, God met with Moses up close and personal, to convey His intentions for the Israelites, who would be His chosen people on earth. These laws were straight forward. Do this, don't do that... Inevitably not every scenario was covered but God's intentions were made clear. "Love God supremely and love your neighbor as yourself" was the 30,000 foot view. There were plenty of details in the laws given to Moses, but every situation would be unique, so the Jews had to figure out how the laws applied to their special problems. After the book of Exodus, God gave further instructions in the book of Leviticus. A special tent of meeting was to be erected and worship services were enacted. God had many specific directions for His worship. Next in the book of Numbers, God commanded Moses to number the people, and he reviewed the wanderings of Israel in the desert. By the time we get to the book of Deuteronomy, nearly 40 years have passed since the plagues and the crossing of the Red Sea. The original Israelites who came out of Egypt had all perished except for Joshua and Caleb. It was time too for Moses to pass on into glory, but He was compelled to once again review with the people the law of God. Interestingly the emphasis of this teaching is the care and concern God has for His people and how it is in their best interest to follow it completely. Also there was a stern warning that there would be curses to punish the people if the law was not followed. The book of Deuteronomy also reviews the essential commands that God gave to Moses on Mt. Sinai.

As the centuries went by, Jewish teachers (Rabbis) felt the need to explain and fill-in needed details so people would know how to obey God. Thus, the people were taught a collection of rabbinic interpretations along with the direct commands from God to Moses. This body of knowledge grew and grew, and it was passed down orally from each generation.

These oral traditions were a rehash of the history of Israel down through the ages, added to by the new rabbi on the scene. Of course the new rabbi was interpreting current events in view of his historical perspective. In addition to the history being recapped, the law was preserved in this way as well. The rabbi recounted the law and cases which became precedent for all sorts of traditions which sprang up around Jewish life.

These oral traditions became the backdrop of Jewish cultural and religious life during the time of Christ and the apostles. Thus, when we study the Gospels in the New Testament, the religious leaders sometimes asked Jesus about the actual Law which God gave Moses, but they sometimes ask Jesus about these traditions and their bearing on true spirituality.

Jewish Oral Traditions at the Time of Christ

During the time of Christ, the educated and powerful Jews knew the Law given to Moses, but they were also very concerned about obeying these oral traditions of how people were supposed to apply the Law to each situation. There are many references to these traditions, such as in Mark chapter 7 below.

(For the Pharisees and all the Jews do not eat unless they carefully wash their hands, thus observing the traditions of the elders; and when they come from the market place, they do not eat unless they cleanse themselves; and there are many other things which they have received in order to observe, such as the washing of cups and pitchers and copper pots.) The Pharisees and the scribes asked Him, 'Why do Your disciples not walk according to the tradition of the elders, but eat their bread with impure hands?' And He said to them, 'Rightly did Isaiah prophesy of you hypocrites, as it is written: "This people honors me with their lips, but their heart is far away from me. But in vain do they worship me, teaching as doctrines the precepts of men." Neglecting the commandment of God, you hold to the tradition of men.' He was also saying to them, 'You are experts at setting aside the commandment of God in order to keep your tradition.'"

Mark 7:3–9

Christ realized the true purpose of the law was different from what the Jews were practicing. During His ministry He was in constant conflict with them about the traditional interpretations people added to the Law. Often the educated Jews forgot that loving God and loving others are the foundational commands on which all the other commands were built. Christ regularly healed people on the Sabbath, and the Jews had a major emotional crisis over this issue. They had built an entire cultural system around following the traditions, and they missed the real point of having rich and precious relationships with God and others. As the Jews failed to live up to their own moral standards, it created tension in their lives.

Tensions Abound Over Moral Conflicts

...in that they show the work of the Law written in their hearts, their conscience bearing witness and their thoughts alternately accusing or else defending them..."

Romans 2:15

In his treatise to the Romans, Paul takes the first seven chapters of the book to develop the idea that all mankind is without hope as they stand before a holy God. He addresses the godless man in chapter one and the moral man who has a set of values in chapter two. The verse above is a description of the internal role play of the moral man. He realizes that he is not living up to his own moral standards. God has created us to be moral creatures and given us a conscience which acts as our moral compass. This is the situation of the moral man of chapter two. His problem is that his compass is broken and untrustworthy. As he evaluates his thoughts and actions, he realizes that he is failing to live up to his own moral standards.

Two Reactions to the Same Problem

When the moral man, who tries to follow his feeble conscience, fails he has one of two reactions.

First Reaction: He accuses himself; he gets mad at himself. He agrees that he has failed. This is painful because he is faced with self-condemnation and possibly condemnation from others. He feels guilty which leads to emotions of worthlessness, anger and ultimately, depression.

Second Reaction: The alternative reaction is for the moral man to defend himself. This defense usually takes the form of comparing himself with others. As he compares his moral actions with the actions of others, he invariably finds people who fall even further below his standards of behavior. This comparison makes the moral man feel OK because he isn't so bad after all. He thinks a lot of people are far worst. This second reaction can start a vicious emotional cycle. Before long, the person is in a state of mental, emotional and moral confusion. The person's pride tries to find a reason to feel secure and righteous, when in his inner-heart he knows that he has nothing to be proud of.

Real spiritual stability is never realized in either of these reactions. In the first situation, the person just feels guilty and depressed. In the second situation, the person keeps making excuses that other people are doing even worst things. As a result, righteousness is never achieved and forgiveness is never received. Inner peace is never found.

Instead of falling back into our old human habits of comparing ourselves with others we should accept the payment Christ made for us on the cross and bask in our new standing with God: Forgiven, even though we don't deserve it.

Christ our Righteousness

> For Christ is the end of the law for righteousness to everyone who believes.
>
> **Romans 10:4**

Christ's awareness of this breakdown in relationships and man's emphasis on ritual and traditions brought Him to the need to correct it. The new covenant, which we are so familiar with now, was a radical and incomprehensible notion when first introduced. The new covenant made it possible for all mankind to be set free from their broken conscience which binds all people to a cycle of guilt and/or pride. It replaces the broken conscience of the moral man and the missing conscience of the godless man with the Holy Spirit of God, who is perfect in every regard.

Rivers of Living Waters

Jesus came to help us escape from both wrong reactions mentioned above: feeling guilty/depressed and feeling self-righteously proud because some people are even worse than us. Notice what Jesus says in the following Gospel passage:

> He who believes in Me, as the Scripture said, 'From his
> innermost being will flow rivers of living water.'
>
> John 7:38

Jesus promises to give us a vital source of energy to help us live in freedom and inner peace. This energy is from God Himself in the form of the Holy Spirit living in our hearts and lives. The Holy Spirit will be like a well which never runs dry. He will always be available as a source of life-giving water. No longer will we be burdened by depressing guilt or prideful self-deception. God will give the necessary strength and nourishment to anyone who wants it.

Lay Aside the Old Self and Put on the New

> … in reference to your former manner of life, you lay aside
> the old self, . . . that you be renewed in the spirit of your
> mind, and put on the new self. . . .
>
> Ephesians 4:22–24

We have hope. The Apostle Paul explains that we can live victoriously over any sin or temptation. With God's help, we can find deliverance from ANY sin or ANY behavioral problem that enslaves us. We can't overcome such problems on our own, but we can experience victory as we chose to take advantage of God's supernatural power. We need to make a conscious effort to lay aside our old life, habits, and lifestyle, to ask God to help us think correctly about our circumstances.

Examples

Paul succinctly gives the principle in Ephesians 4:22–24, but gives us examples of this principle in verses 25–32. I won't take up space in this volume to print the verses for you, but I encourage you to

Many Possible Besetting Sins

There are many other possible besetting sins. They are too numerous to list them all here. You know what your particular problem or combination of problems are. Ask God to help you think through your motivation for indulging in the sin. Ask God to show you passages in the Bible which will help you grapple with the truth. Also, set up a mechanism to remind yourself regularly of the truth and actively pursue the opposite behavior to the besetting sin. Whenever possible, get a committed Christian friend to support you in forming new habits. With God's help, little-by-little you will retake the ground you have given up to the devil and the flesh.

Coming Up Next

In the chapter ten, I will give you some examples of increasing your godliness by linking hearts and lives with others who have a pure heart to follow Christ and the Bible's teachings about righteousness and godliness. Few experience this fantastic opportunity. Will you be one of the blessed few? I hope so.

For a free video summary of this chapter by the author go online to www.dirtysecretsdirtylies.com and click on Free Videos.

10

Pursue Godliness with Those Who Have a Pure Heart

Not the Lone Ranger...Part of a Family

When God created the universe and the human race, he obviously set up the family as the foundational building block for growing and nurturing people. When Christ started His ministry he set up an additional relational structure called the church. It was a new concept and radically different from anything that was in existence. In Scripture, the church is described in several ways. Sometimes it is called a family or "the household of God."

> So then you are no longer strangers and aliens, but you are fellow citizens with the saints, and are of God's household,
> **Ephesians 2:19**

Isn't that a comforting thought? Christians are part of God's family. Being part of a family has special privileges. Also, family members have special relationships. God wants us to be as committed to other Christians as if we were "blood relatives"—as if we were brothers and sisters.

> But Jesus answered the one who was telling Him and said, "Who is My mother and who are My brothers?" And stretching out His hand toward His disciples, He said, "Behold My mother and My brothers. "For whoever does the will of My Father who is in heaven, he is My brother and sister and mother."
>
> **Matthew 12:48–50**

How about your spiritual family? Do you have one? Is your church like a spiritual family to you? Or, is it more like a club or institution? God intended it to be like a large family with some older and younger brothers and sisters. Are you actively involved with your spiritual family? Are you being an older brother or older sister to a new believer? God wants us all to play a part.

Families Are Not Perfect

Just as there are no perfect families, there are no perfect churches. All the members of our spiritual family are in the developmental process. Some are new believers and some have trusted Christ for decades. Even though all are at varying stages of development, we all need to seek to have pure hearts. God puts a special value on the believer with a pure heart.

> Blessed are the pure in heart, for they shall see God.
>
> **Matthew 5:8**

People who are pure in heart have devoted themselves to God. They love God, and they allow God to teach them and guide their decision. God is looking for people who will give their whole hearts to Him. These "pure in heart" or "wholehearted" people get special support from God.

> For the eyes of the LORD move to and fro throughout the earth that He may strongly support those whose heart is completely His. You have acted foolishly in this. Indeed, from now on you will surely have wars."
>
> 2 Chronicles 16:9

To keep a continuously pure heart, we need to link our hearts with others who have a pure heart. If you have ever been around such wholehearted Christians, you know they sincerely love God and others no matter what level of maturity they have attained. They may not know the details about how to be effective on every level or how to act godly in every respect. One thing they know is to seek God. They call on him with a pure heart. They want all of God. They are wholehearted in what they pursue. They will, given enough time, grow up to become the strong man or woman of God–as He intended.

Those are the people we need to seek out. We need to have our spiritual antenna up for them, so they will be detected. We need to ask God to lead us to them and open up an opportunity to get close to them. Once we find them, we need to follow these instructions:

> Now flee from youthful lusts and pursue righteousness, faith, love and peace, with those who call on the Lord from a pure heart.
>
> 2 Timothy 2:22

Your spiritual development will be directly related to the time and energy you put into pursuing these godly characteristics and shunning youthful lusts with other like-minded believers. There are no "Lone Ranger" Christians. God intended for us to reach our full potential as we pursue Him together with others.

The early church was more than an organization. It was an organism. It was a living, growing, vibrant body of Christ which was extremely interested in knowing God and making Him known to the whole world. The early church met in large groups and from house-to-house. They fellowshipped together, were taught by their leaders, prayed together, and had meals together as they remembered the Lord in the breaking of the bread. These small groups became the crucible of life in which the real Christian growth happened. These house churches were clustered wherever believers lived. They became synonymous with loving one another and bearing one-another's burden.

Not Just a Family a Team

Pursuing like purposes and goals are the building blocks of effective teams. Jesus knew the value of teamwork. He worked hard to make his twelve disciples into a team—and into family. When His mother and brothers came to see him in Luke 8:19–22, they were just visiting. They were not really part of His ministry. Jesus realized their level of commitment was very low. He highly valued the ones who were following Him and the sacrifice they were making. When His biological family came to merely visit, Jesus said,

> "My mother and My brothers are these who hear the word of God and do it."
>
> **Luke 8:21**

This group of true believers had a special place in Christ's heart. They were with Him throughout His earthly ministry even up to the last hours during his capture. That night in the garden of Gethsemane, we get a glimpse into Christ's true vision for the disciples as He prays to His heavenly Father for them.

I have manifested Your name to the men whom You gave Me out of the world; they were Yours and You gave them to Me, and they have kept Your word. Sanctify them in the truth; Your word is truth. As You sent Me into the world, I also have sent them into the world. For their sakes I sanctify Myself, that they themselves also may be sanctified in truth. I do not ask on behalf of these alone, but for those also who believe in Me through their word; that they may all be one; even as You, Father, are in Me and I in You, that they also may be in Us, so that the world may believe that You sent Me.

John 17:6, 17–21

Chapter 17 of John is so important and so beautiful; you must study it for yourself. It gives such deep insight into the way Jesus feels about his people. I hope you will take the time to do an in-depth study of John 17, because it will help you see the type of relationship He intends for us to have with one another and with Himself. In the section quoted above, it is easy to see that God had sent Christ on a mission. Also, we see that Christ is sending them and all the other disciples who will come later on a mission to reach the world with the Gospel. It is such a difficult and important mission that Jesus was compelled to pray for them and all the future disciples who would be involved in it. At first glimpse you would expect that He would detail all the character qualities and skills they would need to possess. Instead Christ merely asks God to "sanctify them in the truth." He also asks the Father to make them into one. What an unusual request. He understood the power of the truth (as we have discussed in this book) and strength of being united, functioning as a team. This world will never be reached without a team effort. We've got to be part of the team, if we are going to be most effective. My question to you is, "Have you bonded with a team of believers with pure hearts and pursuing God's objectives?" If not, you are not in your correct spiritual environment. Christians grow and mature in fellowships with other wholehearted Christians. Here are some passages which show how the early Christians were knit together as a team to accomplish God's purposes.

These all with one mind were continually devoting themselves to prayer, along with the women, and Mary the mother of Jesus, and with His brothers.

Acts 1:14

So Peter was kept in the prison, but prayer for him was being made fervently by the church to God.

Acts 12:5

Mission

Only conduct yourselves in a manner worthy of the Gospel of Christ, so that whether I come and see you or remain absent, I will hear of you that you are standing firm in one spirit, with one mind striving together for the faith of the Gospel;

Philippians 1:27

These inspiring words were penned by one of my personal heroes, the apostle Paul. After he was confronted by Christ on the road to Damascus in Acts 9, Paul was never the same. In chapter 9, he begins his earnest quest of making Christ known to the entire world. As committed, excited, and educated as he was, Paul realized that he could not accomplish his mission alone. Even from the earliest days of his ministry, Paul teamed with others knowing that he could multiply his efforts if he worked with others. In Acts 13, he worked together with Barnabas for their first missionary journey. Great things happen on that trip with several churches started and a strong foundation for the advance of Christianity toward Europe.

Picking up Paul's story later in the book of Acts, in chapter 19, we find that he and a small team of leaders, made their way into the Roman state of Asia (currently the western part of Turkey). He entered Ephesus, which at that time was the capital of Roman Asia. For a period of approximately three years, Paul stayed in Ephesus and went to work reaching the lost and building the church there. In three short years, Paul and his team reached not only the city but the entire region of Asia (See Acts 19:10). Paul taught the Christians in this area the same truth: work as a team. Paul prays that the believers were,

> "…standing firm in one spirit, with one mind striving together for the faith of the Gospel."
>
> **Phil. 1:27d**

Are you on a team like that? … One heart, one mind, striving together for the faith of the Gospel? If not, you need to find such a group of saints, so you can link hearts, arms and lives and accomplish the mission Christ has given us.

For a free video summary of this chapter by the author go online to www.dirtysecretsdirtylies.com and click on Free Videos.

11 Visualize the End from the Beginning

It's Supernatural

The whole process of transformation is supernatural.

...that He who began a good work in you will perfect it until the day of Christ Jesus.

Philippians 1:6b

A Life Transformed

When Josie was a young girl, she learned from her parents' example that a person can use lies to manipulate those around her. Josie's ability to convincingly lie often worked, but it also got her into trouble from time to time. When she was in her mid-twenties, she moved into a new neighborhood and met Andrea. Andrea was radically different from the people Josie had known in the past. Andrea lived her Christian faith, and Josie was so intrigued that she wanted to do everything Andrea did, even attend her church. Soon, the Lord captured Josie's heart. God's conviction in Josie's heart was so powerful that she knew she had to forsake all the sins in her life, but she didn't know where to start. Josie turned to Andrea for advice. Andrea gently helped her see that God values the truth, and she suggested practical ways for Josie to overcome her lying habit. Little-by-little God transformed her from manipulating people with lies to the kind, gracious person He intended.

God is actively transforming us into the people He intends us to be all along. If this was a secular handbook for character development, I would give you a one, two, three step approach. I would merely ask you to go out and do your best. Instead, God is working in your life to transform you into the image of His Son. Only God can perform this transformation, but He can and will do it using His means and methods. He visualizes the end result of this process in your life and is working all the circumstances to bring it to pass.

Predestined to be Conformed to the Image of Christ

An example of this principle is found in Paul's letter to the Romans:

> For those whom He foreknew, He also predestined to become conformed to the image of His Son...
>
> **Romans 8:29a**

Not only is it God's will for us to overcome whatever besetting sin we face, God is orchestrating our very circumstances to enhance His desired outcome. He brings circumstances to pass and uses them as instruments to mold our lives according to His eternal purposes. Once we understand that life doesn't just happen, but that God is the one behind whatever we are facing, then the whole picture of our lives begins to come into focus. Here is an example:

Unexpected Circumstances at 17

Joni Eareckson Tada was paralyzed at age 17. Since that day, she has been a quadriplegic, paralyzed from the shoulders down. She has spent most of her life in a wheelchair, but God used her pain to draw her to Himself. She says, "It is a glorious thing to know that your Father God makes no mistakes in directing or permitting that which crosses the path of your life. It is the glory of God to conceal a matter. It is our glory to trust Him, no matter what."

What's Your Perspective?

Too often we jump to conclusions too quickly. For example, we might look at a picture and decide what it means, but maybe we made our judgment too quickly. Sometimes we judge people on first impressions–and we make big mistakes. This same kind of misinformed conclusion happens when we interpret our circumstances without careful reflection–and particularly when we do not include God's wisdom in trying to understand our lives. When we step back a few steps and consider the great scheme of things, usually our circumstances are interpreted differently. What once was seen as merely an inconvenience or deterrence to our goals might actually be a great blessing.

God Understands the End from the Beginning

Even though our perspective is limited, God's view can either be panoramic or detailed as He wishes. Sam and Jodi were recently married. He wanted to be the best husband he could, so he decided to ask his friend, James, some advice. James had been married for over 30 years and was a wonderful example to follow. James and Sam read through Ephesians 5:15–33 together. James really opened up the passage to

Sam. He gave Sam some practical examples of how he could serve, lead, and shepherd his wife. Over the years, Sam learned much from James' example and the scriptures they studied together. James' experience as a husband and father allowed him to see the bigger picture.

Where God is Taking Us

> All Scripture is inspired by God and profitable for teaching, for reproof, for correction, for training in righteousness, so that the man of God may be adequate, equipped for every good work.
>
> 2 Timothy 3:16–17

The transformed Christian is described as a person who is made adequate and equipped for every good work. For the average reader the word adequate doesn't pack much punch, but Paul intended much more power than our English translation expresses. The Greek word, ἄρτιος, means to be fitted, suited, completed or perfectly satisfying its intended purpose.

Thus, God wants to make us fully ready to do whatever we need to do. The phrase, "equipped for every good work," describes the Christian who has been trained, furnished and practiced in doing the work God as assigned for him or her. Not only are we prepared to accomplish God's goals, we are fully equipped for success. You see, God's intended purpose is for every believer in Christ to reach this point of maturity and effectiveness.

Growth Takes Time

Joey and Philip were friends years ago when Philip was a new believer. Philip's faith was strong, but his life showed many "leftovers" from life of living without God. After a while, Joey moved out-of-state, and they lost contact with each other. Fifteen years later, Joey moved back to his hometown, and the two old friends got to know each other again. Joey discovered that Philip had over the years gotten involved in a thriving church, submitted himself to the Lord's growth process, and had become a strong Christian, a godly husband and father. What an amazing blessing it was to Joey to see how God had transformed Philip life. Just like Philip, we all take time to be transformed. Be patient God is at work but it's worth the wait.

God's Word Does a Work in Us

Remember 2 Timothy 3:16–17 above, this development process happens as the believer interacts with the inspired word of God… that is the Bible. The process of interacting is outlined in four functions described as follows:

Teaching – The Word is to be taught by older, more mature Christians. This practice of teaching was not a new concept when Paul discussed it. The Old Testament prophets were widely known as teachers. One of the first documented teachers was Moses. Much of his teaching is found in Deuteronomy and other early Old Testament books. Of course, our Lord Jesus Christ had an extensive teaching ministry which was well documented. As church history unfolds we find that the apostles' teaching was an important staple of Christian development as denoted in

> They were continually devoting themselves to the apostles' teaching …
>
> **Act 2:42a.**

Teaching is the general pronouncing of God's truth to believers usually with general examples. Rarely does the teacher give specific instructions to individuals to single them out.

Consistent Teaching Make a Huge Difference

For the last fifteen years, Sandi has been involved in a home-based Bible study group with some friends where she received sound Biblical teaching. After all those years, now she has a grounded knowledge of the truth. She enthusiastically told her friend, Penny that she learned to love the Scriptures during those times of instruction. Like Sandy, we all need to regularly learn from godly, effective and sound Bible teachers.

Reproof – The Greek word, ἔλεγχος, translated reproof means to prove or point out in order to prove or correct. Usually this process of pointing out explicit error in Christian virtues is done on an individual person-by-person basis.

Correction – Correction is a normal outcome of reproof. As an individual Christian is reproved with God's truth, he or she will need specific guidance on what to do in the future.

God Uses the Ones We Are Close To

Janice and Molly were good friends. They both loved the Lord and they were both married with young children. Both of them had many opportunities to grow in patience, as mothers of young children often do. But that's where the similarities ended. Janice allowed God to work through her trials to help her to become more and more patient. Molly, on the other hand, allowed her struggles with her children to create resentment and anger. One day while chatting, Janice told Molly about how she was noticing God's work in her life and how she was realizing that she had more patience now. In addition, Janice commented that God was helping her to let go her old habits of becoming angry. At first, Molly was annoyed with Janice. After a few minutes she began to think through the things her friend had said. She realized that acting on her anger with her children and was not honoring to the Lord. She also noticed how upset it made the children. She remembered how much harder the kids were to manage when she was angry with them. With that, Molly chose to be humble herself about her shortcomings and learn from her friend's example and gentle correction.

Training in Righteousness

Jorge had a problem with cussing. He did not notice it, because he was around people who cursed on a regular basis. The words just seemed to bubble up from inside him. But he realized that he had a problem. He didn't want to abuse his Lord's name, so he took practical steps to train himself into a new habit. He bought a 3x5 card and wrote a reminder to himself: "Speak something encouraging and give thanks." Now, every time he is tempted to cuss, he pulled out his card and reviewed it. He has a practical training tool that has helped him build a new habit that honors the Lord.

The Greek word translated training is παιδεία. As demonstrated in the example above, this training is not merely the correction process, but is the entire training and educational process. It encompasses the development of a spiritual understanding and as well as the development of godly character and godly habits. This is a term used of the training of athletes to be experts in their sport.

In Christianity today, teaching is a widely used form of ministry, but reproof and correction are very seldom used. There is even less training in righteousness and godliness. Is it any wonder that there are so few believers who have reached God's intended outcome of being grown up into all aspects of Christ and effectively useful in Kingdom work?

Clearly, God had these purposes in mind when He inspired 2 Timothy 3:16–17. We need to study this passage and actively apply its principles to our lives. Enough instruction given here, now it's time for a case study which brings out all these principles.

Case Study—Reproof, Correction and Training in Righteousness

> If your brother sins, go and show him his fault in private; if he listens to you, you have won your brother. But if he does not listen to you, take one or two more with you, so that 'by the mouth of two or three witnesses every fact may be confirmed.' If he refuses to listen to them, tell it to the church; and if he refuses to listen even to the church, let him be to you as a Gentile and a tax collector.
>
> **Matthew 18:15–17**

Richard's anger was a defining part of his life. It primarily came out in his speech. He had never hit his wife, Anne, but he had often railed at her with until she cried. His words cut deep like a knife into her very soul. His coworkers also feared him because of the barbs he would let fly at any provocation.

He and his wife had been involved in their church for years, but Richard's habit of tongue-lashing had created many rifts with friends there. Craig, one of Richard's friends at church, was very concerned about Richard and decided to talk to him about his outbursts of anger.

Privately, Craig went to Richard and spoke to him about his abusive speech. Richard became very angry and blasted Craig for bringing up the subject. Even though it was hard, Craig was very patient with Richard and responded in kindness. Richard told him to get out of his house and never come back. Craig left and prayed about what he should do next.

He came back again in a few days with his pastor, Stan, and another man from the church. Very belligerent, Richard reacted to their visit by shouting at them and cursing them. Stan was the spokesman for the group and tried to reason with Richard. It just made him madder. Stan reminded Richard that God said we are to put away malice and hateful speech in Colossians 3:8 and Ephesians 4:31. Richard was not willing to change his attitude. In fact, he continued to attack all the men and demanded that they leave.

The three men left. After they left they discussed the situation and asked God what to do next. As they prayed the Lord reminded them of the passage in Matthew 18 listed above. They felt under the circumstances they had no other choice but to let the church know what had happened and suggest that Richard be removed from church fellowship. At that point, Richard was unwilling to admit his sin of railing and turn away from it.

The next Sunday Richard and Anne were not at church. The three men were deeply grieved over the situation. They told the church what had happened with Richard a few days before and everyone was in shock. After some discussion, the entire congregation realized that they had allowed the situation to go on too long. They felt the only scriptural solution was to remove Richard from their church fellowship.

Someone pointed out that it was best for Richard to see that there were consequences to his sin. They prayed together for him, and they all realized how serious unchecked sin is. That day the church leaders got together and wrote a short letter to Richard about the action which had been taken against him. They reassured him that they cared about him, but that his attitude and actions must change. They also pointed out that God would be supernaturally dealing with his rebellion and that it would be very difficult. They told him that He could expect God to work against him until his life turned around.

A day or two later Richard got the letter. His initial reaction was a fit of rage, but he knew deep down inside that his leaders were right. His stubborn pride would not allow him to admit he was wrong. For months he fumed about the action.

As time went by, things turned out just like the letter said. Nothing was going well for Richard and Anne. Richard let his temper get away from him one day at work and cussed out his supervisor. After a review by the human resources department, he lost his job. Without a job, and not being able to draw unemployment compensation, they went through their savings very quickly. After a few months they were on the verge of bankruptcy. In desperation, Richard stormed out of the house and sped off in his car. Crying uncontrollably, he began to curse God for allowing these terrible things to happen to him. That was the first time in months he had even spoken to the Lord. After he drove for a few minutes, he stopped at an embankment and said to himself that he would just run the car off into the water and end all his misery.

Then suddenly, he sensed the presence of the Lord. It was as though the Lord was saying to him. "Why don't you forsake your pride, humble yourself and I'll take care of things for you?" Richard's immediate response was, "Lord, how can I? I've gone too far." Just at that time he looked down on the floor of the car and noticed his Bible. There was a letter sticking out of it. Richard felt compelled to pick it up. it was the letter from his church leaders. Richard had stuck it in his Bible after he got it and angrily thrown his Bible under the car seat. The Lord had safely kept it there all this time so that just at the right time, Richard would have it.

Richard pulled out the letter and re-read it. He realized that it wasn't as bad as he remembered it. It actually sounded like his leaders really did care about him and wanted to help him overcome his anger. He asked the Lord if this is really the solution to his problem.

Suddenly, a peace came over Richard like he had never experienced before. He read the letter again and again. It got better every time he read it. He even looked up the verses in Matthew and found that Jesus really did give those instructions. Finally, he prayed, "Lord, I'll do anything you say. Please give me the strength I need."

He turned the car around and went home. Anne met him at the door, she was sure something horrible was going to happen to him when he left the house in such a rage. When he came in, he fell down on his knees before her and said, "Honey, I've said and done so many hurtful things to you, can you ever forgive me?" Those were the most wonderful words she had ever heard. She threw her arms around him, and they both sobbed. They both asked God to forgive them and resolved to let Christ be Lord of their life.

After a few hours had passed and much discussion, Richard and Anne decided together that they needed to call Stan, their pastor, and ask forgiveness. They did and Stan came over with the other leaders. Richard told them everything that had happened and asked forgiveness. Of course the leaders were thrilled. The next Sunday, the leaders brought Richard and Anne before the congregation and Richard was restored to the church.

Richard had made a great decision to follow Christ, but it wasn't always easy to follow through with his decision. Slowly, old habits were replaced by new godly habits of kindness, patience, and self-discipline. God was faithful and true to him. Over time and with continued training, Richard became a mighty man for the Lord Jesus Christ.

Perhaps We Should Reconsider

This well-known outline found in Matthew 18 above is rarely practiced by Christians today. We do not take this command seriously. But, we need to be ready to reprove, correct, and train each other. Because so few Christians implement this directive, we are not seeing most Christians fully living out their potential. It doesn't make sense that we will get the desired godly results when we do not follow God's instructions.

Goal of Redeeming Mankind

From eternity past, God had the redemption of mankind on His heart. He was not caught off guard when Adam and Eve disobeyed in the Garden. He knew that His creation, with their free will, would ultimately have a moral failure. Being a just God, that moral failure must be punished. That moral failure would result in the perfect opportunity for Him to demonstrate His divine attributes outside of a theoretical framework. He could model His perfect justice, His endless mercy, His unfathomable love, His undeterred patience and His infinite Grace in the redemption of His most brilliant and complex creation, mankind.

This plan of redemption was carried out by His most precious possession, His very own Son, the Lord Jesus Christ. During His time on earth, Jesus was completely consumed with the business at hand. The following passage reveals Christ's intensity about His purpose even at an early age:

And He said to them,

Why is it that you were looking for Me? Did you not know that I had to be in My Father's house?'

Luke 2:49

As Jesus' ministry moved into its later years, He was approached by some Pharisees in the following passage. When He declared that they should send a message to Herod for Him that he was not afraid of death, He displayed once again His single purpose:

And He said to them,

Go and tell that fox, 'Behold, I cast out demons and perform cures today and tomorrow, and the third day I reach My goal.'

Luke 13:32

Throughout Jesus' life He never lost His vision for His life, but even translated that vision into practical plans and goals which brought the vision to fruition.

Vision Takes the Eyes of Faith

Let me give you another example which shows the power of visualization. For years I was a homebuilder. Usually the future home owner had a vision of her dream home long before the architect even drew the first sketch. She could imagine the bedrooms with her children joyfully playing, the kitchen where there was an active circle of friends and family gathered to prepare the Christmas meal, the den where everyone would sit near a cozy fireplace, and, of course, the dining room table where daily life and future dreams would be discussed. She could visualize her home through the eyes of faith.

Just as the future home owner visualizes her completed home, the Christian should visualize his or her life as a mature, victorious Christian. Our hope will be fulfilled and the first step is imagining the goal and the second step is starting the process we have described earlier in this chapter.

God Spoke the World into Existence

Then God said, 'Let there be light;' and there was light.

Genesis 1:3

As we discussed in Chapter Six, God spoke and His will came into existence. We are similar to God and we can also speak our future into existence as we visualize the end through the eyes of faith. I recall many in the past who would say, "One day... I'll have my dream home." In the same way, we Christians must affirm God's outcome for our lives as we exercise faith.

Up Next

In chapter twelve I will help you realize that there are some significant obstacles to your success. Your faith will fail unless you face them and overcome them.

For a free video summary of this chapter by the author go online to www.dirtysecretsdirtylies.com and click on Free Videos.

12

Why You
May Fail

Sometimes We Fail Because of Unbelief

Stephanie was 25 and felt she her biological clock was ticking. She really wanted to be married and have a family before she got too old. She had had a few relationships with guys, but those guys were always shallow or selfish or something else. You know... selfish jerks who usually told her what she wanted to hear, to get what they wanted. For years, Stephanie has wanted to get married and have a family. The problem was that she didn't ask God for help and guidance. She just kept responding to anyone who would give her the attention she craved. As time went by she began to open up about her real feelings to her close friend Kayla. After discussing her situation for some time, Kayla asked her a penetrating question. "Do you believe God has a plan to meet your needs for a husband and a family?" That was the first time that Stephanie realized that she did not believe that God was really interested in love and family life. After she considered it for a few minutes, she had to admit, "I don't really believe God will do that for me."

Obstacles of Faith

There are many roadblocks which hinder the growth of our faith. Jesus tells us in John 5:44 that one of the primary obstacles of our faith is seeking the approval of other people and not seeking God's approval.

> How can you believe, when you receive glory from one another and you do not seek the glory that is from the one and only God?
>
> **John 5:44**

Of course this is a rhetorical question at its finest. Our level of faith is directly related to our personal motives and our desire to glorify God. So, we need to ask ourselves: "Who are you trying to please? ...People, your parents, your authorities, your peers, yourself?" Obviously one of the biggest obstacles to faith is not seeking to please and honor God above all else.

Who Does God Notice?

So what did Stephanie in the story above need to do? Who was she trying to please? Certainly she was seeking to please herself. Who should she try to please? God, of course. Would she have gotten His attention had she sought to gain His approval by her attitudes and actions? Consider the passage below.

> Thus says the LORD, "Heaven is My throne and the earth is My footstool. Where then is a house you could build for Me? And where is a place that I may rest? For My hand

made all these things, Thus all these things came into
being," declares the LORD. "But to this one I will look, to
him who is humble and contrite of spirit, and who trembles
at My word."

Isaiah 66:1, 2

Do you want God's approval and attention? This passage tells you
how to get it.

One Coin, Two Sides

This obstacle is like a two sided coin. If unbelief is one side of the coin,
pride is the other side. Wherever there is unbelief, there is always pride.
In Stephanie's story above, she did not have faith that God would provide
the husband she needed, so she took matters into her own hands. Her
pride might not be noticed, but it is found in her belief that she can
control her life and that solve her problems according to her own rules.
She did not understand the Biblical dynamic that, as mentioned in
Isaiah 66 above, God goes into action for the humble person who trusts
(faith) Him with whatever circumstances he or she is facing. Peter states
this important principle in another way below:

and all of you, clothe yourselves with humility toward one
another, for GOD IS OPPOSED TO THE PROUD, BUT GIVES
GRACE TO THE HUMBLE.

1Peter 5:5b

There is another coin as well. One side of that coin is faith and the
other side is humility. Faith and humility work together and they invite
God's grace and favor. God will resist our pride and unbelief. Clearly the
position of Grace is where you want to be.

Faith Comes from Hearing

In order to develop our faith there are a few things we need to do. The following verse helps us to start understanding this next principle.

> So faith comes from hearing, and hearing by the word of Christ.
>
> **Romans 10:17**

Brandon had become very discouraged in his relationship with his boss. It seemed that every idea he presented to his boss was immediately rejected. He knew he had some great ideas which would really improve job productivity and effectiveness, but he never could get his boss to even consider the changes. After several attempts to communicate these things to his boss, he no longer believed that he could be successful. In desperation, with humility he confessed to the Lord that he was not able to persuade his boss about these changes, and he needed help. He asked God to give him the insight into how to effectively communicate these ideas. A few days went by and no ideas came to him. Fortunately, he was contacted by Andrew, an old Christian friend from college for a lunch appointment. Catching up over lunch, Brandon shared the roadblocks he had encountered with the boss. Andrew understood Brandon's frustrations, but he also knew how to apply God's word to the situation. He shared what he had recently learned from 1 Timothy 5:1.

> Do not sharply rebuke an older man, but rather appeal to him as a father, to the younger men as brothers,
>
> **1 Timothy 5:1**

Because of Brandon's humility just a few days before, God answered his prayer for wisdom by sending Andrew to share this principle of persuasion. Immediately Brandon's faith increased as he heard the word of Christ.

Sometimes We Fail Because We Don't Remember What God Has Done for Us in Past

Oh, what short memories we have. This reminds me of the story of the Israelites in Numbers chapter 14 and 15. We do not have time to go through every verse of this story in this section of this book, but read these two chapters soon. God had brought the nation of Israel out of Egypt miraculously through a series of events which demonstrated His ability to deliver them through any circumstance. This is normal. God usually gives individuals and whole generations of people tests to demonstrate their ultimate faith in the Lord and His promises. This was such a time for the people of Israel. God was ready to move this generation into the land of Canaan and deliver on His promises. God gave them every opportunity to take Him at His word, enjoy His promises, and experience the grace of God. God also gave leaders the opportunity to guide the people into God's perfect plan. But, they rejected God's plan. How simple it would have been for them to merely remember what God had already done for them and use that as a springboard for believing in their present test.

Psalms 78 recounts the events in Numbers 14 and 15 with additional comments on the continuing unbelief of the Israelites up to the time of King David. In contrast to the Jewish people's forgetfulness of God's goodness, young David had a good memory. When David faced Goliath, he remembered how he had trusted God in his battles with the lion and the bear (See 1 Samuel 17:32–37). Those memories gave him courage and faith to believe that God would deliver him from the hand of Goliath.

How has God supernaturally worked in your life? You might sit down and make a list of times God has guided you through hard times.

Now, think: Isn't He faithful enough to help you through whatever you are currently facing? One of the keys to faith is proactively remembering and reviewing the ways God has been faithful to you and helped you in the past.

Wrong Kind of Self-Talk

In chapter seven, we discussed that what we say to ourselves can bring changes in our lives. In this section, we will return to this theme and look at an example of the wrong kind of self-talk.

David had been promised the kingdom by Samuel earlier in his life. He had seen many victories where it was smooth sailing such as the slaying of Goliath and the numerous army battles which were victorious. After much success, God allowed David's faith to be tested when King Saul became increasingly jealous of David success and popularity. Saul repeatedly tried to murder David. Saul's irrational rage and paranoia lead him to continually hunt for David and to try to kill him. Through it all God repeatedly delivered David. Finally, after so many attacks, David forgot about God's faithfulness, and David said to himself,

> Now I will perish one day by the hand of Saul. There is nothing better for me than to escape into the land of the Philistines. Saul then will despair of searching for me anymore in all the territory of Israel and I will escape from his hand."
>
> **1 Samuel 27:1**

With these words David began a journey of unbelief which lasted about 18 months. During that time, David actually helped the enemy – the Philistines.

What we say to ourselves really does matter. Our words both reflect what we believe, and they can guide us to have a new set of beliefs. Be very careful about what you say. It will probably come true.

Sometimes People Hinder Our Faith

In addition to how we influence ourselves with our inner conversations, we also need to be careful about outside influences. The doubts created by other people can be some of our hardest obstacles to living in joyful faith. Our friends might quietly discourage our faith. People we look up to because of their knowledge or years of experience might create doubts. These people are doubters. It's not that they totally disagree with what we know to be true; they just don't know for sure. They take away our confidence in little ways. They say things like, "I'm not so sure about that." Or, "You should get some advice about that before you go off the deep end." One step beyond the doubters is the cynics. These are the people who belittle your faith. They reduce your faith to an absurdity and make you feel worthless and stupid. The Bible calls these people "revilers." They are verbally abusive. They say things like, "You're an idiot if you believe that." Or, "You probably also believe that pigs can fly." Another negative person is the discourager. They use their words to block you from obeying God. They say things like, "I really think you are going down the wrong path." Or, "You are wasting your time being so concerned about following Christ." All these people must be avoided at all costs. They will wreck your faith and render you ineffective for Christ.

Sometimes We Don't Have Any Mentors

Not only do we need to avoid the doubters, cynics and discouragers who are want to hinder our faith, we must proactively engage with older more godly mentors who have God's and our interests at heart. The Scriptures are full of examples of such positive and wise people helping others do great things for God. Moses trained and encouraged Joshua, Jesus taught his disciples, and Paul guided Timothy and Titus to trust God. If you don't have godly mentors in your life, you will not have the support system you need in order to gain victory. Additionally, it is crucial to have a peer accountability partner along the journey. For more details about this subject refer to chapter ten.

Sometimes Strong Negative Emotions Overwhelm Us

Shame and guilt are powerful forces which can lead to failure. Shame and guilt come when we feel that we are not meeting either our own standard of conduct or the standards of others. Once we do something wrong, we remind ourselves of our fault, and we relive those experiences. As a result, we live in shame and guilt. Let me give you an example. Growing up Alex consistently wet the bed until he was eight years old. He never wanted to do it. He really tied hard not to, but it was beyond his control. It just happened. He was constantly being ridiculed about it. His cousins teased him unmercifully as did his Aunt Margie. The shame and guilt continued through his life. Years later, he still had difficulty forgiving his cousins and aunt. Whenever he was around them, he re-experienced the shame and guilt again. As a result, he developed a great deal of anger and bitterness. Shame and guilt, if not properly resolved, can wreck our lives.

These emotions can lead to several other negative emotions. In the example of Alex above, his shame and guilt lead to anger and bitterness. When Alex needed to see his aunt and his cousins later in his life (like at a wedding or family reunion), he would become fearful, worried and anxious. He did not want to be embarrassed if the subject came up. A long chain of reactions developed because Alex did not know how to guide his feelings of guilt and shame. We can have similar problems if we allow negative emotions to control us. And, those confused feelings will hinder us from conquering the sin that is defeating us.

Sometimes We Need a Bigger "Why" to Motivate Us

Let us look at another example, Maxine had always been overweight. Now she weighed more than ever. She was the proverbial "Big Mama."

Just tipping the scales at 425 pounds, her small 5'4" frame couldn't handle much more. Over the years she had tried diet after diet, but she only regained the weight she lost. Now things were different. She had an appointment with her doctor and in no uncertain terms he told her that her health was at risk. Years of unrestrained eating of unhealthy food, such as fried foods, sugar, caffeine, white pastas, white bread, diet soda, and fast food, had spoiled her health. Her obese body needed healthy food, but it also needed to lose weight. Finally, she realized that she had to make harsh changes in her life.

If you don't believe that the destructive behavior in which you are engaging will greatly damage you and your loved ones, you will not be motivated to overcome it.

Not Big Enough Want to and Commitment

> As the deer pants for the water brooks, so my soul pants for You, O God. My soul thirsts for God, for the living God; when shall I come and appear before God?
>
> **Psalms 42:1, 2**

I've been asked, "How do you change your 'want to'?" "Want to" is a strong emotion. Many things can drive us to want to. Our "want to" is directly related to the motivation of the "why" mentioned above. From the previous story, Maxine did not want to eat less. She enjoyed eating. It brought her pleasure. It wasn't until she had a good reason to change (the answer to "Why change?") that she was motivated. Instead of focusing on changing our "want to", we must focus on the why we should change. Constantly reminding ourselves of the value of the "why" will change the "want to". As the why becomes our central focus it becomes easier to raise our level of commitment to follow through.

Overcoming a besetting sin requires a huge commitment. It's very difficult. You have to be committed to taking up your cross and following Christ. We know with God's help we can make that commitment and fulfill it.

In this chapter I have explored some of the reasons we may fail. The devil and many people around us will try to discourage us from successfully following Christ. Thus, we need to be prepared for the attack, and we need to hold fast to our faith and objectives. In the final chapter, you will learn about others with seemingly overwhelming obstacles to their faith, who have been successful—and you can too.

For a free video summary of this chapter by the author go online to www.dirtysecretsdirtylies.com and click on Free Videos.

13

Others Succeed, You Can, Too

Jordan, the Crack Baby

All the odds were stacked against Jordan from the birth – he was a crack baby. His mother, Tomica, had five other children before Jordan. Tomica was hopelessly addicted to cocaine. All her children had separate fathers, and she was not even sure who Jordan's farther really was. Tomica decided after she had Jordan that she couldn't keep him because of her addiction, so she gave him up. Jordan had many medical issues from birth, most of which came from the fact that he was a crack baby. His mother's use of crack cocaine left his little body craving for the very substance which devastated him. Jordan became a ward of the state at one week old. Who would take care of him; would anyone adopt him? But, God had plans for Jordan. After six years of marriage, Jimmy and

Marci could not have children. After checking with several doctors, they knew that they would never have children. Yet, they still wanted to have a family and started the process of adoption. After qualifying to serve as foster parents, Jimmy and Marcy learned about Jordan. Knowing that he was a crack baby, they decided to trust God's help to give Jordan a normal life. After six months as Jordan's foster parents, they started the process to adopt him. Over the years, Jimmy and Marcy grew to love Jordan more and more. They did a lot of research about how to minister to their special needs child. Through their diligent love and care, Jordan developed and eventually he put his trust in Christ at age six. His parents continued to teach him God's way and ultimately Jordan overcame his crack related issues and became a dynamic, effective Christian leader. Thank God that His grace is sufficient for whatever we encounter.

In Retrospect

Has your life in the past been filled with failure? Are you spending time dwelling on those failures and beating yourself up over them? Are you feeling guilty and ashamed? You'll never be able to completely overcome your sin until you lay the past failures behind. Paul said it this way:

> Brethren, I do not regard myself as having laid hold of it yet; but one thing I do: forgetting what lies behind and reaching forward to what lies ahead,
>
> **Philippians 3:13**

Don't let your past failures define who you will be in the future. Dwell on your victories, even the small ones. Remind yourself of God's guidance and blessings in the past. Believe that, with God's help, you can continue on a victorious path.

What's Next?

Next you must implement the practical steps to freedom from your besetting sin. As outlined earlier in this book, start by visualizing the end from the beginning-keep your goal in mind. This will give you a frame of reference about where you are going. This will also give you hope that you can overcome. Visualize yourself in a tempting situation and imagine yourself asking for God's help and doing the right thing. Thank God that he will deliver you the next time you are tempted.

Next identify the problem so that you will be prepared when it comes. You may be fighting pornography. Remember the pattern of events which make it hard to resist viewing it. Overcoming the temptation might be as simple as excluding certain websites from your browser or only using your computer in a public place.

Then be sure to remember that you, as a lone individual, cannot overcome your besetting sin. you need God's grace. He wants to be your source of power to overcome whatever you are facing.

Also, remember that your victory is directly related to discovering the truth about the temptation and integrating it into your life and will. This is where it is essential for you to develop a set of affirmations which you review and say daily. The Bible teaches us that "Faith comes from hearing and hearing from the word of Christ" (Romans 10:17). Next take action. Substitute the positive actions of godly obedience for your old sins. Changing your actions will automatically change your negative emotions to position ones. In short order, you will begin to experience joy, peace, hope, courage and all the positive godly emotions of the Christian life.

In order to stay on track, build a network of fellow believers who are pure in heart. These true friends will become a constant source of help and encouragement to you. They will inspire you to more consistent godliness and become your most precious friends. Look for an older more mature believer to partner with you – someone who will show you the ropes of the Christian life and guide you. These relationships will make you much more victorious and more fruitful than you could be living as a loner.

Get Determined

You have a huge task before you, but many people have already traveled your path. Do not let yourself be discouraged. And, remember that even our Savior had his own share of temptations and difficulties. As He was facing the last days of ministry, He knew He was making His last trip to Jerusalem to give His life as the ransom for all mankind.

When the days were approaching for His ascension, He was determined to go to Jerusalem; Luke 9:51

This and other passages show that Jesus knew the difficulties awaiting him, but he was determined to follow the Father's plan. He had confidence in that plan. We too must be determined to stay on the course, no matter how difficult it will be.

Get God's Grace

Remember that fighting old habits of sin cannot be done alone. God never intended for us to do it by ourselves. He promised that He would give grace to the humble. Be sure to take advantage of the empowering strength that only God can supply. As you purpose to receive freedom from your sin, seek God's grace and strength.

Make it Happen

I was once asked, "If not you, then who; If not now, then when?" Isn't it time for you to step up, make a commitment to God to follow Him wholeheartedly, now? Go into action, with God's help. He is willing and waiting to help you.

For the eyes of the LORD move to and fro throughout the earth that He may strongly support those whose heart is completely His . . .

2 Chronicles 16:9a

About the author

Ray Traylor is an ordained Christian minister who has been making disciples for Jesus Christ for over 35 years. He has an extensive Christian teaching ministry with tens of thousands of views on YouTube. A Certified Public Accountant in public practice, Ray is the author of *True Riches: A Practical Biblical Guide to Building Wealth*. He is on the Board of Directors of Christian Care Ministry (CCM), a medical-expense sharing and wellness ministry, a principal in Be Sighted Marketing, an internet marketing firm and a principal in Traylor Productions, which produced a film documentary called *Justice and Beyond*. Ray has been happily married to Brenda Traylor for over 30 years, and they have five adult children and four grandsons.

For free video and learning aids
from the author go to
dirtysecretsdirtylies.com

Printed in the USA
CPSIA information can be obtained
at www.ICGtesting.com
JSHW082345140824
68134JS00020B/1899

9 781614 485193